Nature's
World Records

Nature's
World Records

John R. Quinn

LEARNING
TRIANGLE
PRESS

*Connecting
kids, parents, and teachers
through learning*

An imprint of McGraw-Hill

New York   San Francisco   Washington, D.C.   Auckland   Bogotá   Caracas
Lisbon   London   Madrid   Mexico City   Milan   Montreal   New Delhi
San Juan   Singapore   Sydney   Tokyo   Toronto

McGraw-Hill

A Division of The McGraw·Hill Companies

©1998 by **The McGraw-Hill Companies, Inc.**
Published by Learning Triangle Press, an imprint of McGraw-Hill.

Printed in the United States of America. All rights reserved.
The publisher takes no responsibility for the use of any materials or methods described in this book, nor for the products thereof.

pbk   1 2 3 4 5 6 7 8 9 DOC / DOC 9 0 2 1 0 9 8 7

ISBN 0-07-052658-3

Library of Congress Cataloging-in-Publication Data
Quinn, John R.
    Nature's world records / John R. Quinn.
      p. cm.
    Includes index.
    Summary: Briefly introduces some superlatives in nature such as
the largest living thing, the smallest flowering plant, and the
fastest flying bird.
    ISBN 0-07-052658-3 (pbk.)
    1. Zoology—Miscellanea—Juvenile literature.   2. Botany—
Miscellanea—Juvenile literature.   [1. Zoology—Miscellanea.
2. Botany—Miscellanea.]   I. Title.
QH48.Q52   1997
570—dc21   97-39476
                                     CIP
                                     AC

McGraw-Hill books are available at special quantity discounts. For more information, please write to the Director of Special Sales, McGraw-Hill, 11 West 19th Street, New York, NY 10011. Or contact your local bookstore.

Acquisitions editor: Judith Terrill-Breuer

Production supervisor: Clare B. Stanley

DTP production team: Computer artist supervisor: Nora Ananos
                            Computer artists: Charles Nappa, Charles Burkhour, Steve Gellert
                            Page makeup: Jaclyn J. Boone

Designer: Jaclyn J. Boone   QN

Contents

Look for other record holders in the indexes!

Introduction

Mirror, mirror, on the wall, who's the fairest of them all?

People have been interested in world records for a long time. And some people have set records themselves by living the longest or being the heaviest, the tallest, or the shortest. Other people have eaten dozens of hot dogs—buns, relish, and all—in just a few minutes, or sat in trees or on the tops of flagpoles for weeks, just to set a record. Go figure.

World records exist in nature, too. As you turn the pages in this book, you'll see that nature's world records come in as great a variety as those set by humans. And many are much more dramatic. The cheetah, the world's fastest wild mammal, can run far faster than any human. People can drive cars or fly airplanes at world record speeds, but they can't use their own leg-power to run at 65 miles per hour (104 kph)! The tallest human known was nearly 9 feet (2.7 m) tall, but he was a shrimp compared to the 365-foot (111-m) -tall coast redwood tree, the world's tallest living thing.

So let's take a look at some of the fantastic records nature has set—just by being itself. Because you're a human being, you can read about and appreciate these records. Even if you can't run as fast as a cheetah.

Biggest Living Animal

To find the biggest living animal, we have to go to the sea, where water supports great weight.

The blue whale (*Balaenoptera musculus*) is the biggest animal that has ever lived on land or sea. It is longer and heavier than the largest dinosaur.

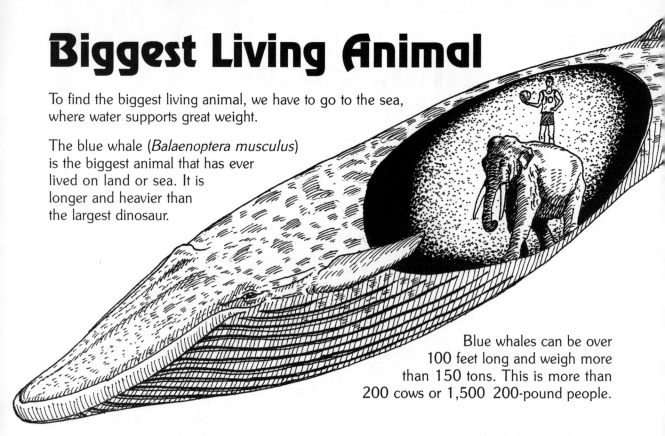

Blue whales can be over 100 feet long and weigh more than 150 tons. This is more than 200 cows or 1,500 200-pound people.

If the whale were hollow, an elephant could stand inside it—leaving enough additional space above it for a basketball player to stand. The whale's heart may be as big as a sports car; its great tongue alone weighs 3 tons (2,700 kg)— as much as a big truck and much more than a large horse.

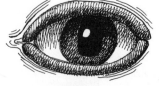

Whale's eye

Human eye

A whale of a baby. Blue whale babies are 25 feet (7.5 m) long—about 4 times the height of a grown man—and weigh about 7 tons when born. They grow at the rate of 10 pounds an hour! This is about 240 pounds (115 kg) per day or 1 ton every 9 to 10 days in their early weeks of growth.

bay-leen-OP-terr-ah MUSS-cule-uss

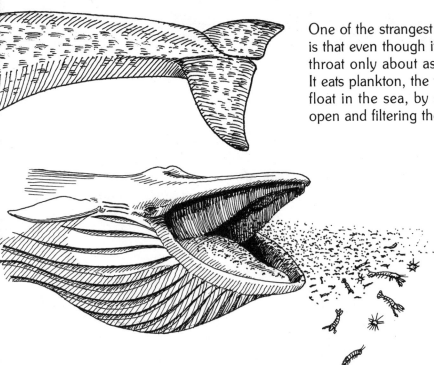

One of the strangest things about the blue whale is that even though it is the largest animal, it has a throat only about as big around as a basketball. It eats plankton, the tiny plants and animals that float in the sea, by swimming with its mouth open and filtering the organisms from the water.

What a racket!
The blue whale's throat may be small, but its voice is big! The whale's strange moaning call is the loudest known animal sound. It has been recorded at 188 decibels, louder than a jet engine (at about 120 decibels)! The whale's voice may be heard underwater by other blue whales as far as 500 miles away.

Scientists think there were about 300,000 blue whales living in the world's oceans at one time. Because so many whales were killed for their meat and oil in the past 100 years, there are less than 10,000 blue whales left alive today. There may be only 200 blue whales left in the whole northern part of the Atlantic Ocean.

The second biggest animal in the world is another whale. The fin whale (Balaenoptera physalus) may be 70 feet (21.2 m) long and weigh about 60 tons. This is a little smaller than Argentosaurus, the largest and heaviest dinosaur we know about. Scientists think fin whales may live between 90 and 100 years.

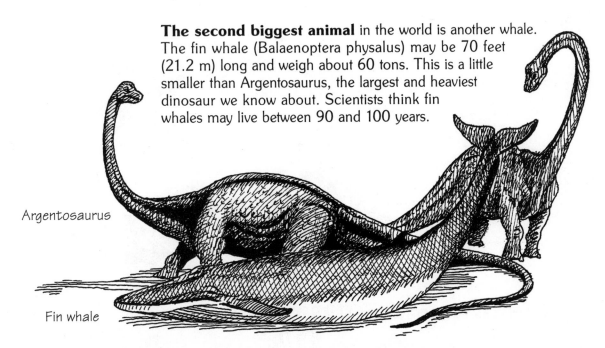

Argentosaurus

Fin whale

Longest Living Animal

The longest animal that we know of is a marine worm called the boot-lace worm (*Lineus longissimus*). These worms often reach 100 feet in length, but the longest ever found was 180 feet (54 m) long! This giant worm must have looked like a living firehose when it washed onto a beach in Scotland after a powerful storm at sea.

linn-EE-uss lonn-JISS-ee-muss

There are about 550 different kinds of marine worms. Most are just a few inches long. They live in shallow water in the world's oceans and are not often seen because they tunnel about in mud.

Biggest Eye

You might think that the world's largest animal, the blue whale, has the largest eye. But this is not true. Its eye is only about four inches long. The big round eye of *Archeteuthis dux*, the giant squid, is the world's largest. It measures over 15 inches (38 cm) across —bigger than a typical dinner plate!

The giant squid's body can be 20 feet (6 m) long and its arms, or tentacles, can reach 35 feet (11.6 m). One giant squid that washed onto a beach weighed more than 2 tons! That's about the same as two full-sized automobiles.

Ark-ee-TOOTH-is ducks

Mystery of the deep. Because these creatures have washed up dead on beaches, we know something about them. But no one has ever seen one alive. Giant squid live in deep parts of the ocean where light cannot penetrate. Scientists think they may swim as deep as 4,000 feet (1,200 m) during the day and move closer to the surface only at night.

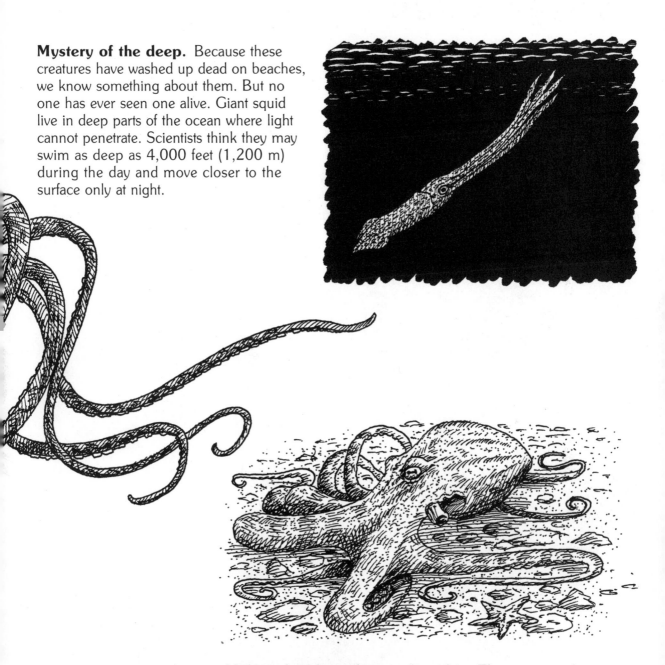

Making heads and tentacles of it. The giant squid is related to the octopuses, but it is much larger than even the biggest octopus. Squids and octopuses are called "cephalopods," which means "head-footed."

Biggest Brain

The biggest and heaviest animal, the blue whale, doesn't have the heaviest brain. That prize belongs to the sperm whale (*Physeter catodon*), which is a smaller animal. Its brain weighs 20 pounds (10 kg)—five pounds more than the brain of the biggest blue whale.

A sperm whale with squid, one of it's favorite foods

What's in a brain? The average adult human brain weighs 3.2 pounds (1.5 kg), so the sperm whale's brain is nearly six times as heavy as ours. But we believe that humans are more intelligent that sperm whales, proving that it's not the size of a brain that counts, but how it has formed and evolved.

Sperm whale spouting

FYE-setter CAT-oh-don

8

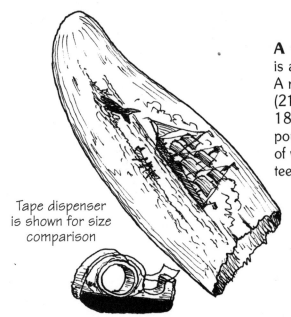

A toothy proposition. The sperm whale is also the biggest living mammal with teeth. A really big sperm whale can be nearly 70 feet (21.6 m) long, and its toothy lower jaw can be 18 feet (5.7 m) long. Its teeth can weigh a pound (450 g) each. People often carve pictures of whaling ships and whales on sperm whale teeth. This kind of art is called "scrimshaw."

Tape dispenser is shown for size comparison

Diagram of sperm whale head

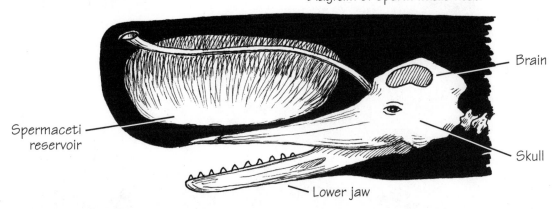

Brain

Spermaceti reservoir

Skull

Lower jaw

A cool head. The sperm whale's huge head takes up one-third of its body length. The whale's head is hollow like a barrel and is filled with an oily substance called "spermaceti."

The sperm whale can make the oil cooler or warmer, so that when it is cool, it becomes heavy and helps the whale dive to great depths. When the whale wants to rise to the surface again, it warms up the oil in its head, which expands and becomes lighter. Then, the whale rises to the surface more easily.

Thar she blows! Most whales and dolphins have two nostrils, or "blowholes," on the top of their heads, but the sperm whale has only one. It is on the front of the whale's big, rounded head and points to the left. When the sperm whale exhales after a dive, its "spout" whooshes out at an angle, not straight up.

9

Biggest Living Fish

Many large fishes live in the sea, but the largest living fish is the 50-ton whale shark (*Rhiniodon typus*), which grows to 60 feet (18 m). It eats plankton in the same way the blue whale does. Even though it is a shark, it has very small teeth. This gigantic fish is so gentle that it will allow a diver to touch it and even grab its tail!

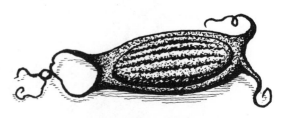

A whopper of an egg. The whale shark lays the largest egg of any animal. It is a foot (30 cm) long and over 5 inches (12 cm) across! The whale shark baby is about 2 feet (60 cm) long when it hatches from the egg. That's about as long as the average skateboard.

The number two champ. The second biggest fish alive today is *Cetorhinus maximus*, the basking shark. This big shark may reach 35 feet (10.7 m), and its huge mouth can open wide enough to swallow a dolphin. These sharks are found in warm oceans all over the world.

RINE-eo-don TYE-puss

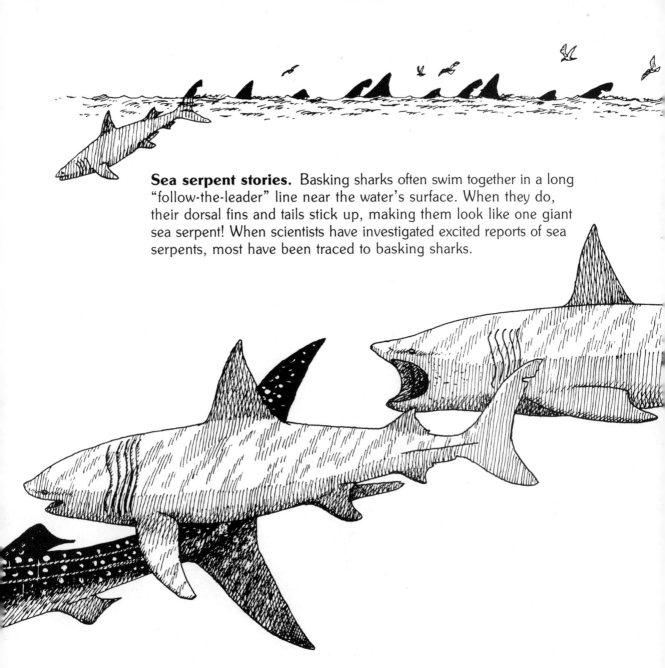

Sea serpent stories. Basking sharks often swim together in a long "follow-the-leader" line near the water's surface. When they do, their dorsal fins and tails stick up, making them look like one giant sea serpent! When scientists have investigated excited reports of sea serpents, most have been traced to basking sharks.

No tough guy. Although *Cetorhinus* is a shark, it is not dangerous. Like the whale shark, this creature has tiny teeth so it cannot eat large animals. Instead, the basking shark has delicate strainers in its gills which are used to filter tiny animals from the water as it swims.

A basking shark swimming along with its mouth wide open looks frightening, but it never attacks other larger creatures, including human divers.

Smallest Living Shark

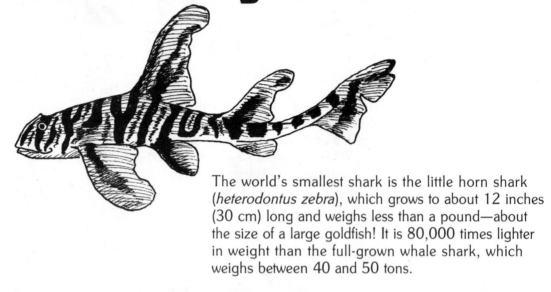

The world's smallest shark is the little horn shark (*heterodontus zebra*), which grows to about 12 inches (30 cm) long and weighs less than a pound—about the size of a large goldfish! It is 80,000 times lighter in weight than the full-grown whale shark, which weighs between 40 and 50 tons.

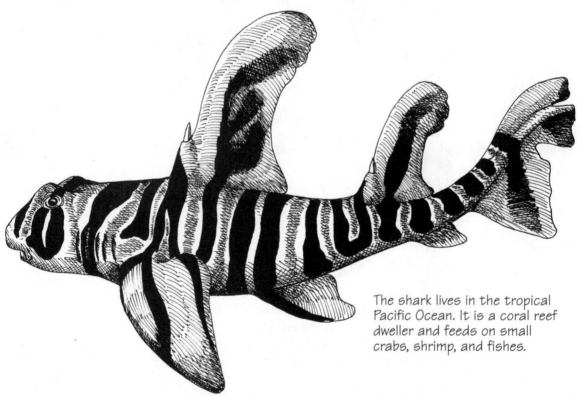

The shark lives in the tropical Pacific Ocean. It is a coral reef dweller and feeds on small crabs, shrimp, and fishes.

het-er-oh-DON-tuss zebra

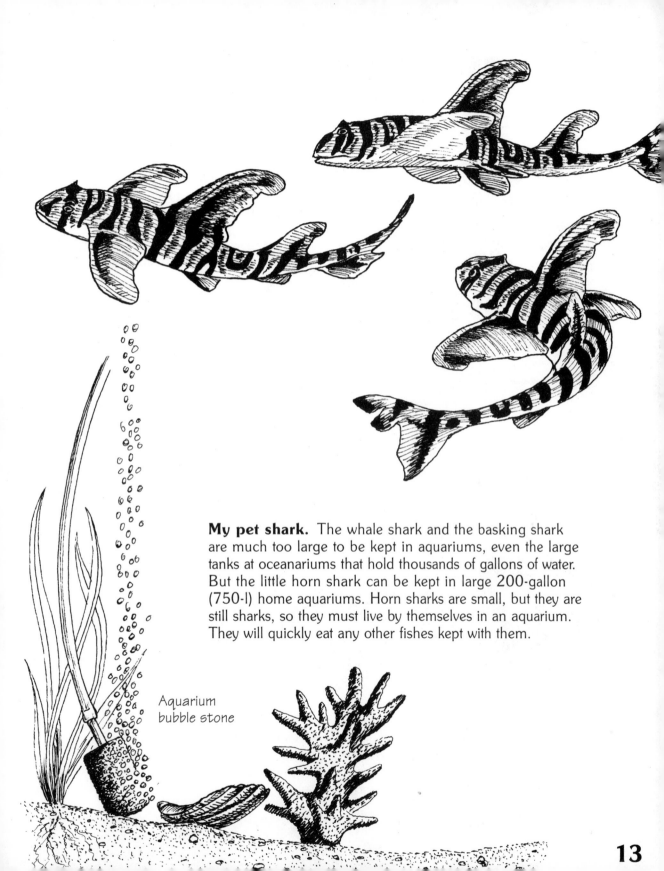

My pet shark. The whale shark and the basking shark are much too large to be kept in aquariums, even the large tanks at oceanariums that hold thousands of gallons of water. But the little horn shark can be kept in large 200-gallon (750-l) home aquariums. Horn sharks are small, but they are still sharks, so they must live by themselves in an aquarium. They will quickly eat any other fishes kept with them.

Aquarium
bubble stone

Biggest Living Carnivorous Fish

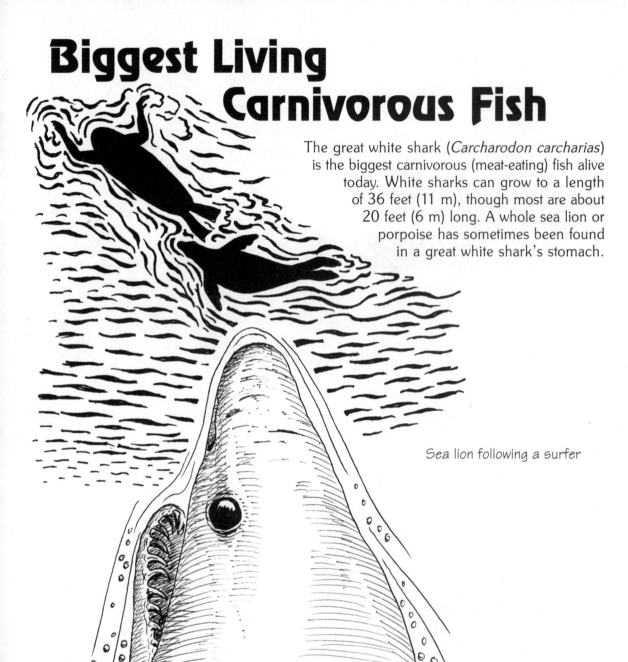

The great white shark (*Carcharodon carcharias*) is the biggest carnivorous (meat-eating) fish alive today. White sharks can grow to a length of 36 feet (11 m), though most are about 20 feet (6 m) long. A whole sea lion or porpoise has sometimes been found in a great white shark's stomach.

Sea lion following a surfer

Jaws. The great white shark is definitely dangerous to people, but only if they are swimming in the shark's habitat. Although many swimmers have been attacked and some have been killed by great whites, the sharks rarely eat their human victims completely. Scientists think the sharks mistake swimming humans for their natural prey— sea lions and large fishes. When they realize their mistake, they often end the attack.

car-CHAR-oh-don car-CHAR-ee-uss

A shark's teeth often break off when the fish grabs its prey. This isn't a big deal to a shark because its teeth are not like ours. They are not set in sockets in the shark's jaws but are actually a part of its skin! Shark teeth are specially modified scales. New ones keep growing inside the shark's mouth and constantly move up front as the old teeth wear out or are broken off.

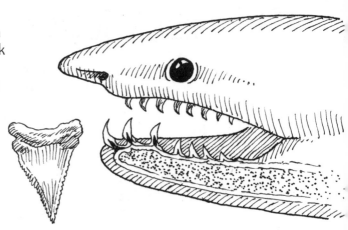

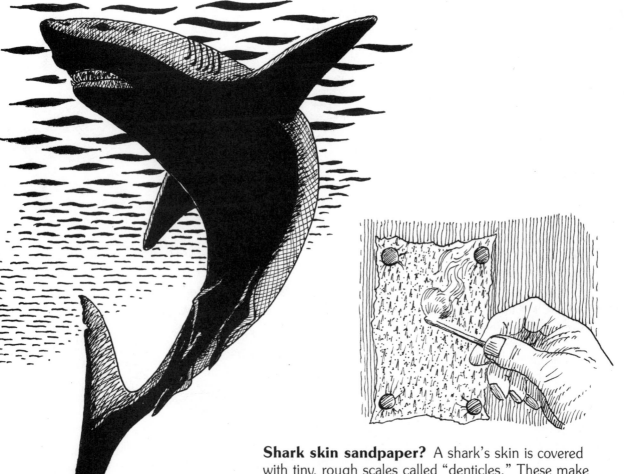

Shark skin sandpaper? A shark's skin is covered with tiny, rough scales called "denticles." These make the shark's body feel as rough as sandpaper. In fact, the dried skin was used as sandpaper many years ago, and boat captains often nailed a small piece of shark skin to the wall of the boat's cabin as a "match striker."

Biggest Shark Ever

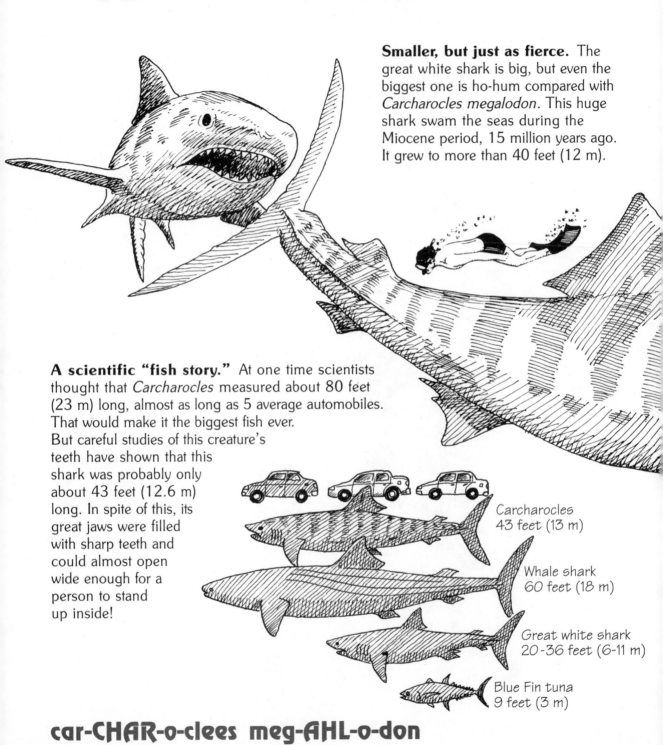

Smaller, but just as fierce. The great white shark is big, but even the biggest one is ho-hum compared with *Carcharocles megalodon*. This huge shark swam the seas during the Miocene period, 15 million years ago. It grew to more than 40 feet (12 m).

A scientific "fish story." At one time scientists thought that *Carcharocles* measured about 80 feet (23 m) long, almost as long as 5 average automobiles. That would make it the biggest fish ever. But careful studies of this creature's teeth have shown that this shark was probably only about 43 feet (12.6 m) long. In spite of this, its great jaws were filled with sharp teeth and could almost open wide enough for a person to stand up inside!

Carcharocles
43 feet (13 m)

Whale shark
60 feet (18 m)

Great white shark
20-36 feet (6-11 m)

Blue Fin tuna
9 feet (3 m)

car-CHAR-o-clees meg-AHL-o-don

An Age-of-Mammals terror. *Carcharocles* lived long after the dinosaurs disappeared from the Earth. In addition to fishes and other sharks, its prey was probably the earliest ancestors of our dolphins and seals.

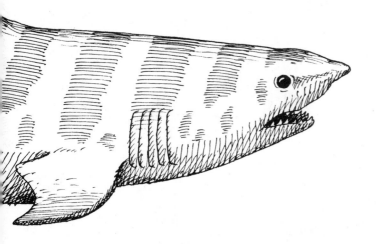

Shark teeth can be many different shapes

Fossil choppers. While most fishes have skeletons made of true bone, the shark's skeleton is made of material called "cartilage." Cartilage is strong and flexible but not nearly as hard as bone. Since cartilage is softer than bone, a dead shark's skeleton usually disappears completely over time. Only its teeth are hard enough to become fossilized, so most shark fossils are teeth only.

Biggest Freshwater Fishes

Fishes that live in fresh water do not grow as large as those that live in the sea—but some can reach an impressive size. The record for fresh water fishes is shared by three species. One is a huge catfish called the Pla Buk (*Pangasianodon gigas*). This fish lives in the Mekong River of Laos and Thailand in Southeast Asia. It reaches 8 feet (2.4 m) long and can weigh up to 360 pounds (162 kg).

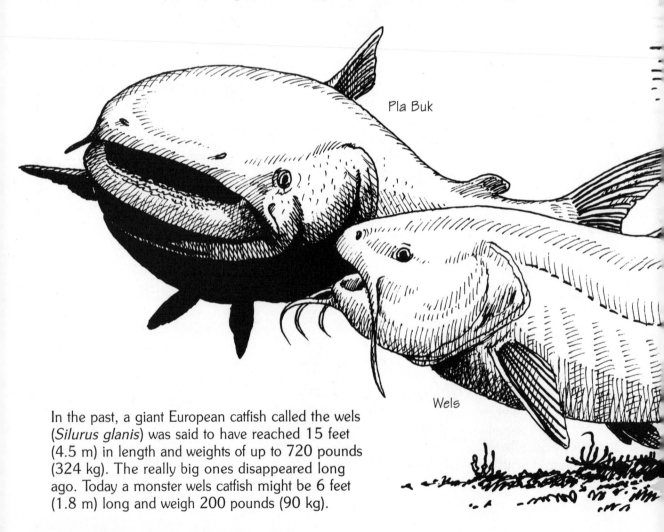

Pla Buk

Wels

In the past, a giant European catfish called the wels (*Silurus glanis*) was said to have reached 15 feet (4.5 m) in length and weights of up to 720 pounds (324 kg). The really big ones disappeared long ago. Today a monster wels catfish might be 6 feet (1.8 m) long and weigh 200 pounds (90 kg).

sy-LOO-russ GLAN-iss

The arapaima, or pirarucu (*Arapaima gigas*) of the rivers of South America is another monster fish that was bigger in the past than it is today. Arapaimas 8 feet (2.4 m) long and weighing 325 pounds (146 kg) were reported in the 1800s. Many have been caught for food, and over the past 100 years, the biggest ones have gotten smaller and smaller. Today the largest arapaimas may be 6$\frac{1}{2}$ feet (2 m) long and weigh about 150 pounds (68 kg).

Arapaima

Biggest Living Turtle

The largest turtle in the world is the leatherback turtle (*Dermochelys coriacea*), which grows to be 9 feet (2.7 m) long and may weigh nearly 2,000 pounds (900 kg). Its great front flippers may stretch almost 9 feet (2.7 m).

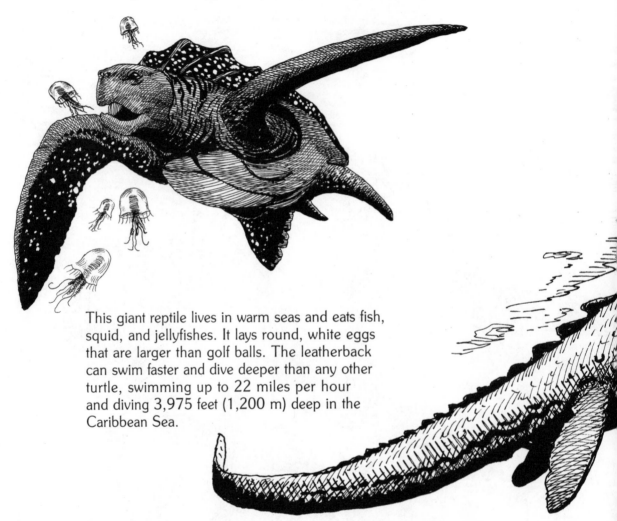

This giant reptile lives in warm seas and eats fish, squid, and jellyfishes. It lays round, white eggs that are larger than golf balls. The leatherback can swim faster and dive deeper than any other turtle, swimming up to 22 miles per hour and diving 3,975 feet (1,200 m) deep in the Caribbean Sea.

derm-oh-KEE-lees kor-ee-AY-see-ah

The leatherback is a real monster but the largest turtle ever was even bigger. *Archelon* was a huge sea turtle that lived about 100 million years ago. It was about 12 feet (3.8 m) long and probably weighed about two tons. A giant swimming reptile called *Mosasaurus* was probably the only predator big and fierce enough to attack and kill *Archelon*.

The leatherback turtle may get sick and die from eating plastic bags floating in the sea. The turtle sometimes mistakes the bags for the jellyfish it usually eats. Because so many leatherbacks have died from eating plastic or from being hit by ships, this turtle is now an endangered species.

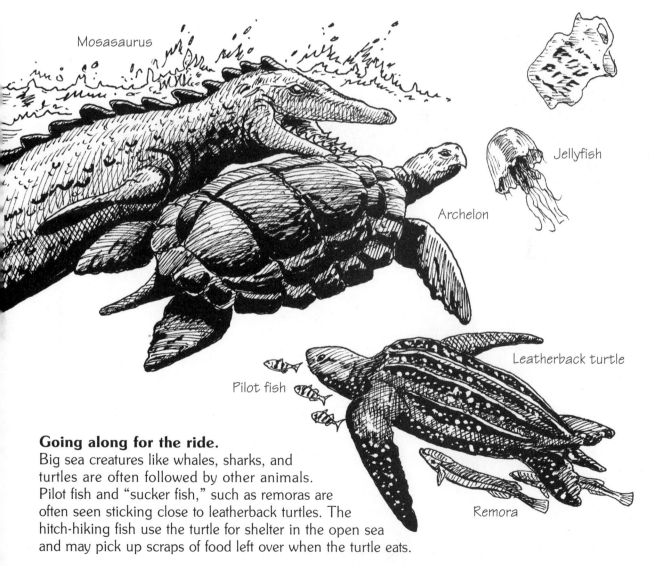

Mosasaurus

Jellyfish

Archelon

Pilot fish

Leatherback turtle

Remora

Going along for the ride.

Big sea creatures like whales, sharks, and turtles are often followed by other animals. Pilot fish and "sucker fish," such as remoras are often seen sticking close to leatherback turtles. The hitch-hiking fish use the turtle for shelter in the open sea and may pick up scraps of food left over when the turtle eats.

Biggest Living Jellyfish

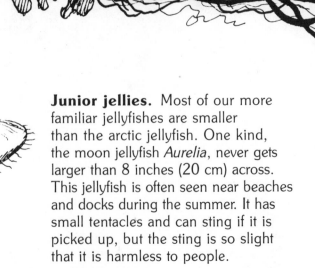

Jellyfish in the sea are usually small. But one kind, the arctic, or sun jellyfish (*Cyanea capillata*), holds a world record for size. The bell, or head, of this jellyfish may be 8 feet (2.5 m) across, and its tentacles can be 200 feet (60 m) long! Fishes and other sea animals are caught with those tentacles and carried into the jellyfish's mouth on the underside of the bell.

Junior jellies. Most of our more familiar jellyfishes are smaller than the arctic jellyfish. One kind, the moon jellyfish *Aurelia*, never gets larger than 8 inches (20 cm) across. This jellyfish is often seen near beaches and docks during the summer. It has small tentacles and can sting if it is picked up, but the sting is so slight that it is harmless to people.

sigh-AN-ee-ya cap-ill-AH-tah

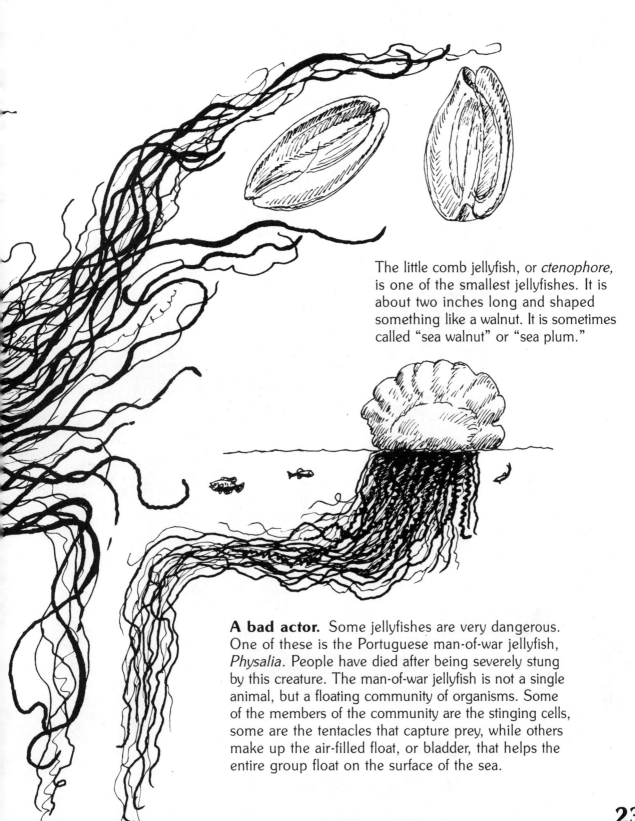

The little comb jellyfish, or *ctenophore,* is one of the smallest jellyfishes. It is about two inches long and shaped something like a walnut. It is sometimes called "sea walnut" or "sea plum."

A bad actor. Some jellyfishes are very dangerous. One of these is the Portuguese man-of-war jellyfish, *Physalia.* People have died after being severely stung by this creature. The man-of-war jellyfish is not a single animal, but a floating community of organisms. Some of the members of the community are the stinging cells, some are the tentacles that capture prey, while others make up the air-filled float, or bladder, that helps the entire group float on the surface of the sea.

Biggest Living Octopus

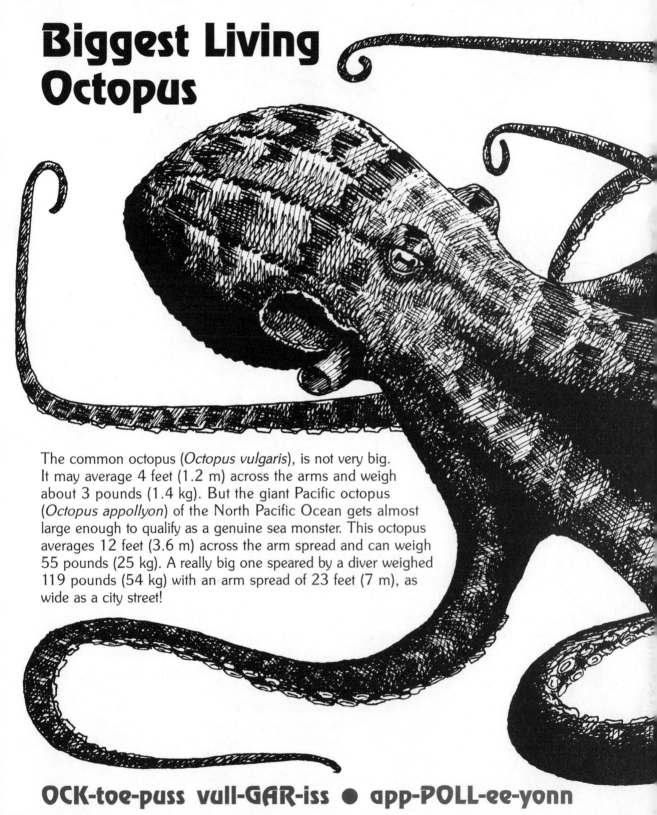

The common octopus (*Octopus vulgaris*), is not very big. It may average 4 feet (1.2 m) across the arms and weigh about 3 pounds (1.4 kg). But the giant Pacific octopus (*Octopus appollyon*) of the North Pacific Ocean gets almost large enough to qualify as a genuine sea monster. This octopus averages 12 feet (3.6 m) across the arm spread and can weigh 55 pounds (25 kg). A really big one speared by a diver weighed 119 pounds (54 kg) with an arm spread of 23 feet (7 m), as wide as a city street!

OCK-toe-puss vull-GAR-iss ● app-POLL-ee-yonn

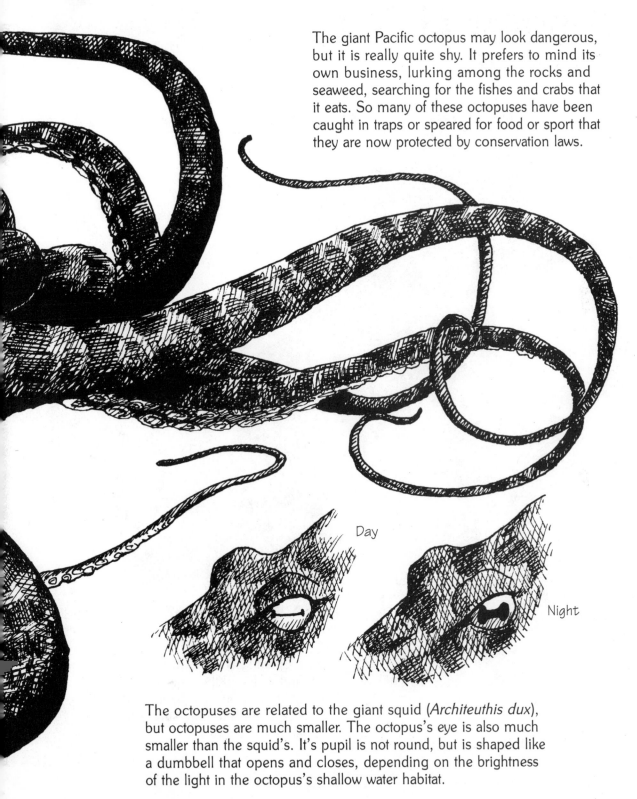

The giant Pacific octopus may look dangerous, but it is really quite shy. It prefers to mind its own business, lurking among the rocks and seaweed, searching for the fishes and crabs that it eats. So many of these octopuses have been caught in traps or speared for food or sport that they are now protected by conservation laws.

Day

Night

The octopuses are related to the giant squid (*Architeuthis dux*), but octopuses are much smaller. The octopus's eye is also much smaller than the squid's. It's pupil is not round, but is shaped like a dumbbell that opens and closes, depending on the brightness of the light in the octopus's shallow water habitat.

Biggest Living Reptile

The islands of the South Pacific Ocean and the shores of Southeast Asia are the home of the biggest reptile in the world, the marine crocodile, *Crocodylus porosus*. It can grow 27 feet (8 m) long and weigh 4,000 pounds (1,800 kg). Crocodiles usually eat large fishes, but one of this size could probably swallow a whole deer or goat.

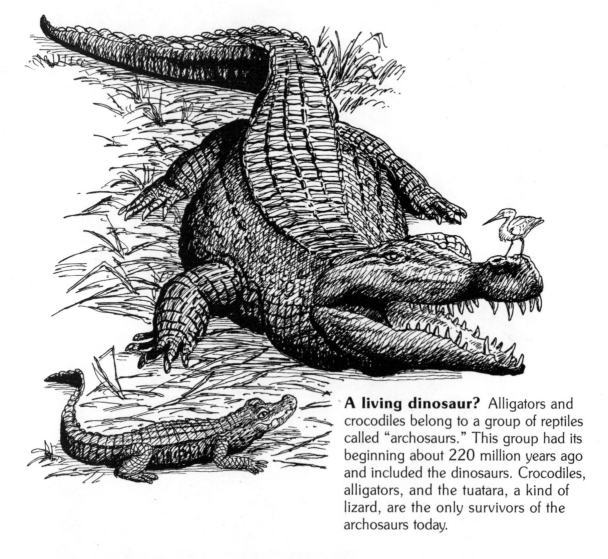

A living dinosaur? Alligators and crocodiles belong to a group of reptiles called "archosaurs." This group had its beginning about 220 million years ago and included the dinosaurs. Crocodiles, alligators, and the tuatara, a kind of lizard, are the only survivors of the archosaurs today.

krock-oh-DIE-luss por-OH-suss

The Pinocchio croc. The crocodile with the longest snout is the gharial, *Gavialis gangeticus* of India. A 20-foot-long (6 m) gharial's jaws may be 3 feet (1 m) long. The long jaws swipe sideways when a fish swims near, and the slippery prey is held securely by the gharial's sharp teeth.

A real love nest. Crocodiles lay about 75 round white eggs in a nest made of damp grass and leaves. The heat of the sun warms the pile of grass and incubates the eggs. When the eggs hatch, the 8-inch (20-cm) -long babies make strange yapping noises. The mother croc then opens the nest so the babies can leave. She may even carry them to the water in her mouth. Little crocodiles may follow their mother about for a week or two before they finally go on their own.

Crocodile tears.
Crocodiles have tear glands just like we do. They help keep the croc's eyes moist when it is out of water. Since the croc's mouth looks like it is always grinning, when its "tears" are dripping from its eyes, it seems to be crying when it is not. So, when we say people cry "crocodile tears," it means that they are only pretending to be sad.

Biggest Living Lizard

The biggest lizard in the world is the Komodo dragon, or monitor lizard (*Varanus komodoensis*). It can be $11\frac{1}{2}$ feet (3.7 m) long and weigh more than 350 pounds (145 kg). Most are about 9 feet (2.7 m) long and weigh 200 pounds (90 kg)—still mighty big.

Box turtle

The Komodo dragon is the largest lizard of all time except for the giant mosasaurs that lived in the sea during the days of the dinosaurs. These huge creatures were early lizards, but they had flippers instead of legs and feet. The biggest mosasaurs reached 50 feet (15 m) long.

Mosasaur
35-50 feet (10-15 m)

Megalania
26 feet (8 m)

Komodo dragon
11 feet (3 m)

VAR-ann-us kom-oh-doe-ENN-siss

A modern-day dinosaur. The Komodo dragon eats deer and wild pigs. It can attack and kill adult water buffalos weighing 1,500 pounds (680 kg)! Occasionally it has attacked people, but in spite of this, it is considered rare and is protected on its island habitats.

It's a long, long tale. The longest lizard in the world is another monitor lizard. The crocodile monitor, *Varanus salvadori*, lives on the island of New Guinea in the Pacific Ocean. The longest one was 15 feet, 7 inches long (4.8 m) from nose to tail. These monitors sometimes climb trees and sunbathe on thick branches.

Tallest Living Thing

The tallest living thing on land is a plant, not an animal, and it is found near the West Coast of the United States. It is a coast redwood tree (*Sequoia sempervirens*) living in northern California. The very biggest has been given a name —it's called, well, "Tallest Tree." It is 362 feet (110.2 m) tall and is 43 feet, 11 inches (13.3 m) around at its base. Several other trees in the forest where "Tallest Tree" lives are now about 360 feet (110 m) tall and may soon set records as well.

This great tree is about 3,800 years old and is as tall as a football field is long. If it were cut down, there would be enough wood to build about 40 small houses. So many redwood trees *have* been cut down that they are now protected in several national and state forests in California.

see-KWOY-ah semp-er-VEE-rens

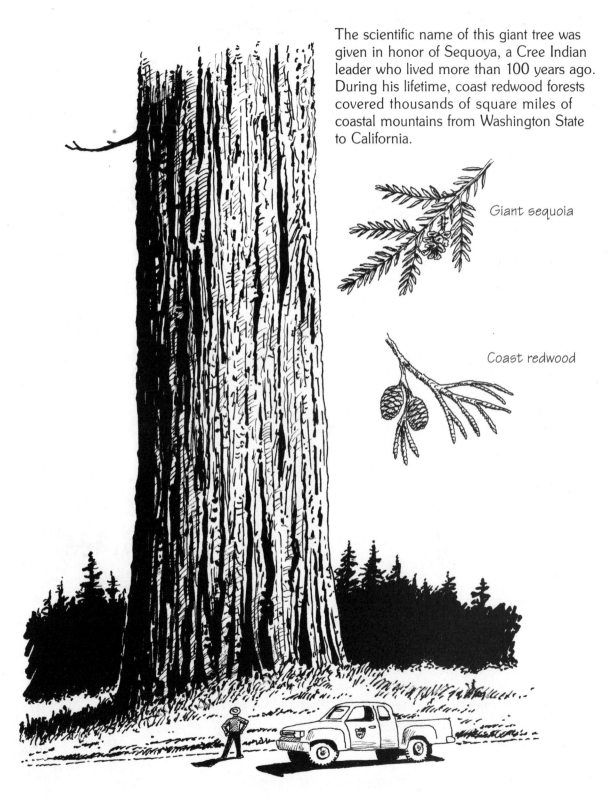

The scientific name of this giant tree was given in honor of Sequoya, a Cree Indian leader who lived more than 100 years ago. During his lifetime, coast redwood forests covered thousands of square miles of coastal mountains from Washington State to California.

Giant sequoia

Coast redwood

Most Massive Living Thing

The most massive living thing on Earth today is another kind of redwood tree (*Sequoiadendron giganteum*), a giant sequoia called "The General Sherman." At its base, this huge tree is 80 feet (25 m) around, which would make it almost as big around as an average suburban house! Scientists have estimated that its total weight, including its roots, is about 6,000 tons, making it about 500 times heavier than the blue whale.

Sequoia leaves and cones

Billions of matches.
"The General Sherman" is about 275 feet (83 m) tall. The "General" has enough wood to make more than 5 billion wooden matches. Its rough, reddish bark is 24 inches (61 cm) thick in some places on the trunk.

SEE-kwoy-ah-DEN-dron   jye-GANN-tee-um

What a difference!
The giant sequoia's seeds are real featherweights, weighing only $\frac{1}{6000}$th of an ounce (4.7 mg). But if the seed sprouts and grows to a mature tree 275 feet (82 m) tall, its weight is multiplied by about 1 billion, 300 thousand times.

Biggest Reptiles Ever

Thunder lizards. The largest and heaviest animals that have ever walked on the Earth were the huge sauropod ("lizard-footed") dinosaurs. They lived during the Jurassic and Cretaceous periods, between 208 and 65 million years ago.

There were many different kinds of sauropod dinosaurs, averaging between 80 and 100 feet (25-30 m) long and weighing from 15 to 100 tons.

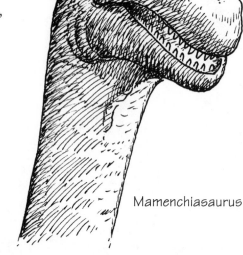

Mamenchiasaurus

Brachiosaurus

Up in the treetops.
The tallest of the sauropods was Brachiosaurus, or "arm lizard." Its head was 46 feet (14 m) above the ground, so it could look down on the biggest T-rex. This dinosaur was about 73 feet (22 m) long and probably weighed about 90 tons. It lived in western North America between 150 and 144 million years ago.

BRAY-kee-oh-SAWR-uss

Sticking your neck out.
The dinosaur with the longest
neck was the Jurassic sauropod
Mamenchiasaurus. Its neck
was 36 feet (11 m) long, as
long as three full-sized cars
parked end-to-end.

Argentosaurus

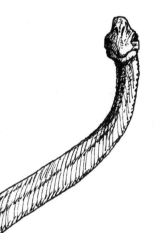

Diplodocus

The tractor-trailer of dinos.
The longest known dinosaur was
the Diplodocus, a giant sauropod
that lived in North America about
130 million years ago. One skeleton
put together from the bones of
several of these great creatures
measured 87 feet, 6 inches (26 m)
long, about as long as 9 compact
cars. Its long, tapering tail alone
was 50 feet, 6 inches (15 m) long.
This skeleton was 11 feet, 9 inches
(3.5 m) high at its backbone.

The heaviest known dinosaur was
probably Argentosaurus, whose fossils
were found in Argentina. Scientists
studying this creature's huge vertebrae,
or backbones, estimated that it weighed
about 110 tons. That weight would
put this dinosaur second only to the
blue whale as the world's heaviest
animal ever.

35

Biggest Land Mammal Ever

The largest land mammal that ever lived looked kind of like a long-necked elephant without a trunk. It was a type of hornless rhinoceros called *Baluchitherium* (also called *Paraceratherium*). It lived during the Oligocene Period of the Age of Mammals, about 35 million years ago.

Baluchitherium stood 18 feet (5.5 m) high at its shoulders and was 37 feet (11.5 m) long, as long as a school bus! It weighed about 20 tons—four times more than any school bus. It probably ate the leaves of tall trees, like giraffes do.

Baluchitherium is known to us only by its "scientific name" because there were no people around 35 million years ago to name it anything else. It was named after the Eurasian country of Baluchistan, where its great bones were first discovered. "Therium" means "beast" in Latin.

bal-oo-kee-THEER-ee-um

Living tanks. The name "rhinoceros" means "nose-horn," and all living rhinos have horns. Rhinoceroses are among the largest and most powerful of mammals. Only very young or injured rhinos are in any real danger of attack by predators.

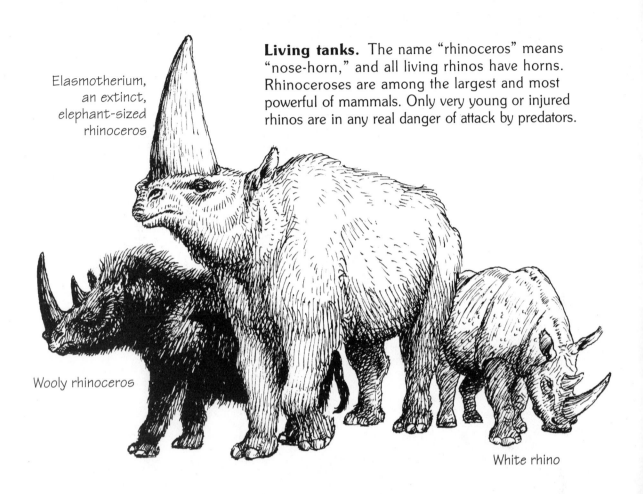

Elasmotherium, an extinct, elephant-sized rhinoceros

Wooly rhinoceros

White rhino

Indian rhinoceros

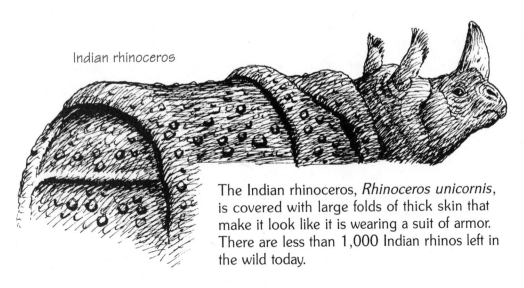

The Indian rhinoceros, *Rhinoceros unicornis*, is covered with large folds of thick skin that make it look like it is wearing a suit of armor. There are less than 1,000 Indian rhinos left in the wild today.

Biggest Living Land Mammal

The world's largest living land animal is the African elephant (*Loxodonta africanus*). A big bull elephant can stand over 12 feet (4 m) high at his shoulders, and the biggest can weigh over 8 tons (10,000 kg), about as much as a large bulldozer. Most large elephants, however, weigh about 4 tons (5,000 kg).

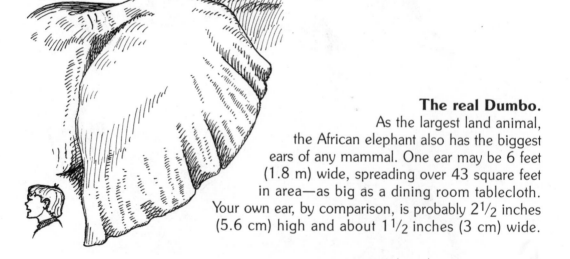

The real Dumbo.
As the largest land animal, the African elephant also has the biggest ears of any mammal. One ear may be 6 feet (1.8 m) wide, spreading over 43 square feet in area—as big as a dining room tablecloth. Your own ear, by comparison, is probably 2 1/2 inches (5.6 cm) high and about 1 1/2 inches (3 cm) wide.

Try wagging that! Elephants have the longest tails of any mammal, too. The Asian elephant's tail is the longest—5 feet (1.5 m) long. Extinct elephants such as mammoths and mastodons had short tails. This is because they lived in cold places where a very long tail would quickly lose body heat and freeze.

Lox-oh-DON-tuh aff-ree-CAN-uss

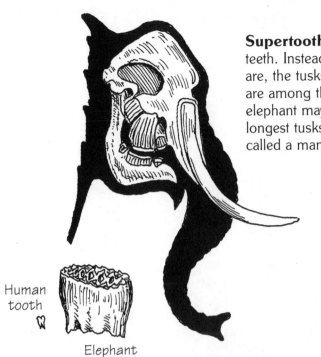

Supertooth. An elephant's tusks are really two of its teeth. Instead of being entirely inside, the way our teeth are, the tusks emerge from the elephant's mouth. They are among the longest teeth in the world! A large African elephant may have tusks 8 or 9 feet (2.5 m) long. The longest tusks on record belonged to an extinct elephant called a mammoth. They were 16 feet (5 m) long.

Human
tooth

Elephant
tooth

Big foot. An elephant's great weight is supported by a fatty pad on the sole of its foot. This spreads the animal's weight evenly so that when elephants walk, they hardly make a sound or leave any footprints.

An elephant's "nose," or trunk, is also king-sized. A big bull's trunk can be 6 feet (1.8 m) long and can hold 15 to 20 quarts of water at a slurp. With its trunk, an elephant can pick up objects as small as peanuts or as large as a tree trunk. The elephant eats about 330 pounds (150 kg) of plants and drinks 50 gallons of water every day.

Both African and Asian elephants are gradually disappearing because the places where they live are being taken over by people. Many are killed for their meat and tusks. Thirty years ago, there were about one and one-half million elephants living in Africa. Today there are less than 500,000.

39

Longest Tusks Ever

Mammoths lived in many parts of the world thousands of years ago. They were ancestors of our modern African and Asian elephants. The mammoths were huge, and so were their tusks. In fact, mammoth tusks are the longest elephant tusks ever found.

A mountain of a mammoth. The steppe mammoth (*Mammuthus trogontheri*) of Europe and Asia was the largest of all mammoths and known elephants. It was 14 feet, 9 inches (4.5 m) high at its shoulder, nearly twice the height of a room ceiling. It lived 300,000 years ago.

MAH-mooth-uss trow-gon-THEER-eye

Tusks like tree trunks. One tusk of a woolly mammoth was 16 feet, 6 inches (5 m) long. That's longer than a full-sized van. The tusks of the straight-tusked elephant (*Paleoloxodon antiquus germanicus*) were almost as long. The tusks of an adult bull were 16 feet (5 m) long. They only appear longer than the woolly mammoth's because they are straight, not curved.

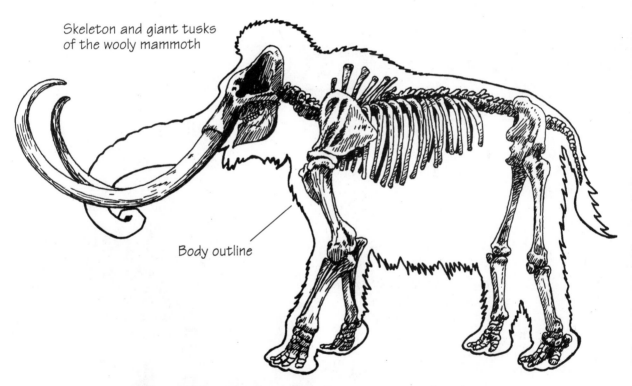

Straight-tusked elephant

Skeleton and giant tusks of the wooly mammoth

Body outline

Mammoth weightlifter. The heaviest mammoth tusk ever found was found in Italy. It weighed 330 pounds (150 kg)— about the weight of a modern refrigerator-freezer. A pair of mammoth tusks weighing 498 pounds (224 kg), about the weight of a truck engine, were found in Nebraska. They were more than 13 feet (4 m) long. Imagine the strength the animal needed just to hold its head up!

41

Biggest Living Land Carnivore

Nanook of the North. The largest meat-eating land animal in the world is the polar bear (*Ursus maritimus*). These giant white "ice bears" can be as long as the former champ, the huge brown bear, and may average 1,300 pounds (600 kg). The largest polar bear ever found was 12 feet (3.65 m) long and weighed 2,210 pounds (1,002 kg)!

Polar bears eat fish, seals, and other animals they can stalk and catch. They also eat any dead animals they find.

The number two bear. The second biggest meat-eating animal in the world lives in Alaska. It is the Kodiak or brown bear (*Ursus arctos middendorffi*). A really big one can be 10 feet (3 m) long and weigh more than 1,800 pounds (816 kg).

ERR-suss mar-uh-TIME-uss

A big set of choppers.
The jaws and teeth of the polar bear
show that it is a carnivore, or meat-eater.
It has large, strong canine teeth like dogs and cats.

No picky eater. Although
the brown bear can kill and eat
animals as large as caribou
(a northern deer), it very often
eats smaller animals like mice,
fishes, and birds whenever it
can catch them. It also eats
insects, fuit, and plants. The
brown bear is very skilled at
fishing and can snatch big
salmon from fast-moving rivers.

Sun bear

House cat shown
for comparison

A real Teddy bear. The smallest bear in the world is the sun
bear, *Helarctos malayanus*, of Southeast Asia. At the most, it
weighs about 100 pounds (45 kg), about as much as a Rottweiler.
Baby sun bears are often kept as pets in jungle villages. Today this
little bear is an endangered species because its forest habitat is
being destroyed and it is still hunted for its meat.

Biggest Wild Cat

Most domestic cats are about 18 inches (45 cm) long and weigh up to 10 pounds (4.5 kg). By contrast, the Siberian tiger (*Panthera tigris tigris*) averages 10 feet, 4 inches (3 m) long and nearly 4 feet (1.2 m) high. A big one can weigh 590 pounds (266 kg)!

pan-THEE-rah TY-griss TY-griss

The Siberian tiger lives in cold northern forests in Russia and Asia and is larger and has much thicker fur than tigers living in warm parts of the world. So many tigers have been killed for their skins or for their body parts that they are endangered. There are only about 200 Siberian tigers left in the wild today.

Siberian tiger cub

Rusty-spotted cat

Miniature poodle

The world's smallest wild cat does qualify as a little kitty. It is the rusty-spotted cat (*Priongilurus rubiginosus*) that lives in the forests of India and Sri Lanka. This little cat may reach 14 to 18 inches (35-45 cm) in length and weigh between $2\frac{1}{2}$ and $3\frac{1}{2}$ pounds (1.1–1.4 kg), about the same weight as a miniature poodle.

45

Biggest Carnivores Ever

For a long time, scientists believed that the biggest meat-eating animal that ever lived was the dinosaur *Tyrannosaurus rex*. Now, they're not so sure. Not long ago, two other giant meat-eating dinosaurs—*Giganatosaurus* and *Carcharodontosaurus*—were discovered that may rival T-rex.

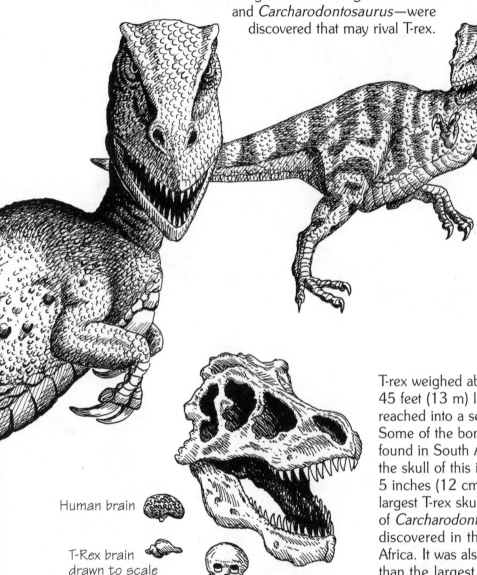

Human brain

T-Rex brain drawn to scale

T-rex weighed about 8 tons and was 45 feet (13 m) long. Its head could have reached into a second-floor window. Some of the bones of *Giganatosaurus* found in South America showed that the skull of this individual, was about 5 inches (12 cm) longer than the largest T-rex skull. Parts of the skull of *Carcharodontosaurus* were discovered in the Sahara Desert of Africa. It was also slightly bigger than the largest known T-rex skull.

jye-GANN-AH-toe-SAWR-uss ●
car-CHAR-o-don-toe-SAWR-uss

So just how big were they? Like T-rex, these big predators were about 19 feet (5.7 m) tall, tall enough to look over the top of a tractor-trailer. Each was about 45 feet (14 m) long and weighed about 9 tons—as much as 9 mid-sized cars.

Carcharodontosaurus, which means "shark-toothed lizard," had curved teeth that averaged 5 inches (12 cm) long. The edges were serrated like the blade of a steak knife, making them fearsome weapons that could easily shear through the toughest flesh. The teeth grew back if they were broken off when the dinosaur bit its prey.

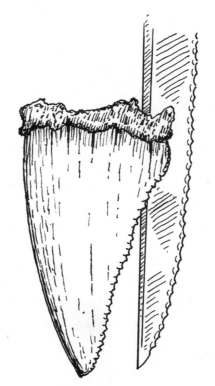

Human teeth shown to scale with T-Rex tooth

The 12-inch-long (30-cm) collared lizard of the U.S. western desert is kind of like a mini-tyrannosaur. Although lizards are not closely related to dinosaurs (except that they are both reptiles), this lizard sometimes runs swiftly on its hind legs like the shark-tooth and T-rex.

"Extinct" Living Fossil

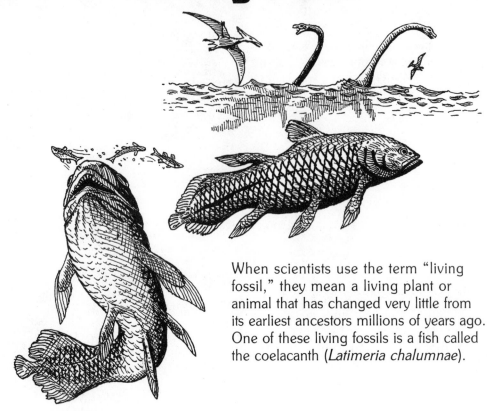

When scientists use the term "living fossil," they mean a living plant or animal that has changed very little from its earliest ancestors millions of years ago. One of these living fossils is a fish called the coelacanth (*Latimeria chalumnae*).

Extinct coelacanth

The coelacanth was discovered in the ocean near Africa in 1938. Before then, people thought these fish had become extinct millions of years ago, during the time of the dinosaurs. The skeleton of the living coelacanth is almost exactly like that of its extinct relatives.

SEE-la-canth ●
latt-ee-MEER-ee-ya chal-OOM-nye

Diagram showing the progression from fish fin to amphibian foot.

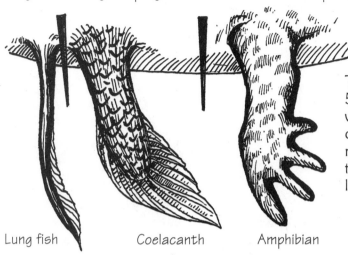

Lung fish   Coelacanth   Amphibian

Today's coelacanth reaches about 5 feet (1.5 m), but one extinct kind was much larger. A coelacanth called *Mawsonia* lived about 100 million years ago. This fish reached the length of 12 feet (3.8 m). It had large coin-like scales all over its body.

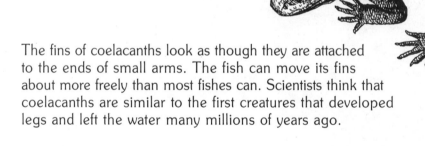

Tuatara

The fins of coelacanths look as though they are attached to the ends of small arms. The fish can move its fins about more freely than most fishes can. Scientists think that coelacanths are similar to the first creatures that developed legs and left the water many millions of years ago.

The tuatara, *Sphenodon punctatus*, or "beak-head" lizard, is another living fossil. It lives on islands near New Zealand. The tuatara reaches 2 feet (60 cm) long and can weigh 5 pounds (2.2 kg). When it scampers over its rocky island home, it breathes hard—it may take one breath every 10 seconds. When it is resting, it breathes about once an hour.

Oldest Fossil

Our earth was formed about 4½ billion years ago, but no rocks that old have yet been found. The oldest rocks on our planet were found in northern Canada. They are nearly 4 billion years old and did not contain fossils.

Stromatolites

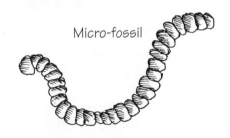

Micro-fossil

stro-MAH-toe-lites

The oldest oldtimers of all. The oldest fossils, found in rocks in Western Australia, are about 3.5 billion years old. These microorganisms are less than a quarter-inch (6 mm) long, making them hard to see without a microscope. They gathered in colonies in shallow water and built large circular mats made of a sticky substance that they produced as they grew. These fossilized mats are called "stromatolites."

Cloudina skeleton

Cross-section

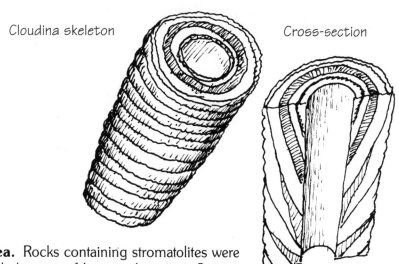

By the beautiful sea. Rocks containing stromatolites were once part of the sandy bottom of bays or lagoons. Over millions of years, the colonies were covered with sand that hardened into stone. Some fossilized stromatolite colonies may cover hundreds of square miles near seacoasts.

Those old bones. The oldest animal skeleton ever found was that of a creature called *Cloudina*. It was a tiny coral animal that lived in the sea near southern Australia about 580 million years ago. *Cloudina's* skeleton looks like tiny ice cream cones stacked inside one another. The skeletons are about 1 1/2 inches (4 cm) long.

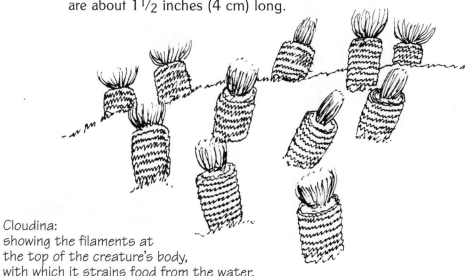

Cloudina:
showing the filaments at
the top of the creature's body,
with which it strains food from the water.

Biggest Living Deer

The world's largest deer is the moose (*Alces alces gigas*), which lives in Alaska and eastern Siberia. It stands almost 8 feet (2.5 m) high at the shoulder, about as high as the ceiling in your room, and weighs about 1,800 pounds (800 kg).

The biggest antlers ever seen on a moose measured 79 inches, almost 8 feet (2.5 m) across. That's about as wide as a large dining room table.

Moose feet are large and spread out—like snowshoes—so it can walk in deep snow. If the moose had small feet like most deer, its great weight would cause it to bog down in snow.

Mouse deer

Bon appetit! The moose has an appetite to match its size. Each day a moose browses about 8.8 pounds of forest plants and 1.9 pounds of water plants. This comes out to about 20,000 tree leaves and 1,100 pond plants.

AL-cees AL-cees GUY-gas

A tiny deer. The smallest deer in the world is no bigger than a rabbit. It is the tiny mouse deer, or chevrotain, *Tragulus javanicus*, of Southeast Asia, which weighs 5 pounds (2.5 kg) and is only about 8 inches (20 cm) high.

Fang fight. The male mouse deer has something no other deer does—long, sharp, canine teeth that are shaped like sabers. Scientists think the tiny deer use them when squabbling among themselves.

The mouse deer evolved 30 million years ago and has not changed much since then. These pint-sized deer are not "true" deer. They are thought to be a link between primitive deer called pecorans and familiar deer such as the moose and white-tailed deer.

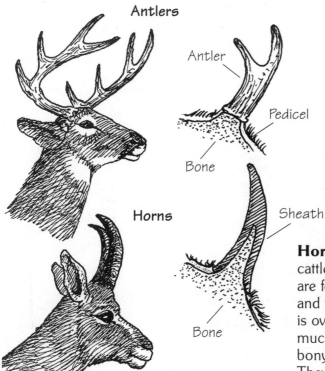

Antlers

Antler

Pedicel

Bone

Horns

Sheath

Bone

Horns or antlers? Deer have antlers; cattle and antelopes have horns. Antlers are formed of solid bone, grow each year, and then drop off when the mating season is over. Horns are made of a hard material much like your fingernails and fit over a bony sheath on the antelope's head. They never fall off.

53

Longest Horns

The longest horns on any mammal are found on the water buffalo (*Bubalus bubalus*) of India and Southeast Asia. One big bull had horns that spread to 13 feet, 11 inches (4.2 m) from tip to tip. This is about as wide as the average living room.

Ankhole

Water buffalo

boo-BAA-luss boo-BAA-luss

The longest single horn was one found on a big bull of a kind of domestic cattle called the Ankhole. It measured $6\frac{3}{4}$ feet (2 m) long. Ankhole cattle are raised for their meat and milk throughout much of Africa.

Texas longhorn cattle of the American West also have very impressive horns. The longest ones ever measured were 9 feet, 9 inches (3 m) across. That's just about as long as the longhorn is from nose to tail.

Rhinoceros

Texas longhorn

Rhinoceros horns can get pretty long, too. A white rhinoceros shot in South Africa in 1848 had a nose horn $62\frac{1}{4}$ inches (1.5 m) long, the width of a full-sized car. A rhino's second horn, called the forehead horn, is usually less than half as long as the nose horn.

Tallest Living Land Mammal

The tallest living land animal in the world is the giraffe (*Giraffa camelopardalis*). One measured 19 feet, 3 inches (5.8 m) tall. Most large giraffes are about 18 feet (5.5 m) tall when fully grown. A grown man can stand up between a giraffe's front legs.

Giraffes live on the plains of Africa and reach up with their 10-foot-long (3-m) necks to eat the leaves of trees. When they drink, they must spread their front legs so that they can reach down to the water.

jeer-AFF-ah cam-MEL-oh-par-DAL-iss

A strong heart. The giraffe's brain is a long way from its heart, and it's all uphill. That means that the giraffe's heart has to be strong in order to pump the blood to the animal's brain. Your brain is only about 18 inches from your heart.

Sticking your neck out. The giraffe, as we know, has a very long neck, but it has the same number of neck bones, or vertebrae, that our necks do. Their 7 neck bones are just a lot longer than ours are.

A real kicker! When giraffes fight among themselves they swing their long necks like battering rams, trying to knock their opponent off its feet. A hard kick by a giraffe can easily kill a lion or hyena!

Baby giraffes are born with their horns on their heads. The horns are small and soft, but they soon harden and stand upright.

Biggest Living Horse

All horses (*Equus cabalus*) are pretty big animals, but some are huge. The biggest of all are the powerful draft horses used to pull wagons and plows. One Belgian stallion measured 6 feet, 6 inches (2 m) high at his shoulder. That's as high as a room doorway. But that horse couldn't get through a door—it weighed 3,200 pounds (1.4 tons), and its mighty chest was 102 inches (255 cm) around.

Shoulder

The tallest horse known was a Percheron from Argentina named Firpon. This horse stood 7 feet, 1 inch (2.1 m) high at the shoulder. He weighed 2,976 pounds (1,350 kg), as much as a cargo van.

EE-kwuss cab-AHL-uss

The heaviest weight ever pulled by horses was 48 tons of logs loaded on a sled. This is about as heavy as five full-sized army tanks. Two Clydesdale horses pulled this tremendous weight 275 yards (248 m) across the snow in Michigan in 1893. The two horses weighed a total of only 3,500 pounds (1,587 kg), less than one-fortieth of the weight they were pulling.

Biggest Living Seal

Big Daddy. The largest seal in the world is the southern elephant seal (*Mirounga leonina*). Adult males can reach $16\frac{1}{2}$ feet (5 m) and weigh 5,000 lbs (2.18 tons). The bulls are much larger and heavier than the slim females, or cows. They measure about 12 feet (3.6 m) around the middle of their body.

The largest elephant seal ever measured was a bull 21 feet, 4 inches (6.5 m) long, weighing about 4 tons. It was killed by whalers in the Falkland Islands near Antarctica.

meer-OON-gah lee-oh-NEE-na

The smallest seal in the world is the Galapagos fur seal, *Arctocephalus galapagoensis*. Female seals may reach 47 inches (1.2 m) in length and weigh 60 pounds (28 kg). The larger males are 60 inches (1.5 m) long and can weigh up to 140 pounds (63 kg).

Wally the walrus.
The walrus (*Odobenus rosmarus*) is another huge seal. A big bull can reach 12 feet (3.6 m) in length and weigh 2,000 pounds.

Seal or sea lion? Seals and sea lions are both members of a group of mammals called "pinnipeds," or "fin-feet." Sea lions are called "eared seals" because they have external ears. They can rotate their hind flippers around and use them to help them run swiftly about on land.

Earless seals have only a small hole on the head where the seal's inner ear is located. These seals cannot rotate their hind flippers forward, so they must hump along on land like giant caterpillars.

Eared seal

Earless seal

Biggest Living Nonhuman Primate

The largest nonhuman primate is the mountain gorilla (*Gorilla beringei*). Adult males can reach 5 feet, 9 inches (1.7 m) tall and weigh 430 pounds (195 kg).

gorr-ILL-ah berr-IN-gee-eye

The smallest nonhuman primate is the very rare pen-tailed shrew (*Ptilocercus lowii*) of Sumatra, Borneo, and Malaysia. The adults reach 5 1/2 inches (138 mm) and weigh only about 1.7 ounces (50 g).

The pygmy marmoset (*Cebuella pygmae*) is a close second for the "smallest primate" title. It is about the same size as the pen-tailed shrew, but it weighs a little more—2.6 ounces (75 g). This tiny creature lives in the rainforests of the Amazon region of South America.

Biggest Living Bat

The Dracula Bat. There are about 1,000 species of bats in the world. Most species are small, with wingspans about the same size as those of small birds. In German, bats are called *fleidermaus*, which means "fluttering mouse." But one kind of bat, the "flying fox" (*Pteropus neohibernicus*) from New Guinea, is much larger than any mouse and all other bats, too. Its wings may spread to 5 feet, 5 inches (1.6 m). The largest flying fox ever measured had a wingspan of 6 feet (1.8 m).

terr-OH-puss nee-oh-hy-BERR-nee-cuss

64

Mini-bat. The smallest bat in the world is the Kitti's hog-nosed bat (*Craseonycteris thonglongyai*) of Thailand. Its wings stretch to 6 1/4 inches (15 cm), and it weighs about 3/4 ounce (2 g). It is so small that it is often called the "bumblebee bat." This bat is now an endangered species because so much of its rainforest home has been destroyed.

Flying by radar. Bats have small eyes and can see well, but they don't rely on their eyesight to find prey at night. They make very high-pitched sounds that bounce off objects and return to their sensitive ears. By measuring how long the sound waves take to come back, the bat can tell exactly how close its prey is.

Bats and mice. Because they have large ears and mouse-like faces, people sometimes think of bats as "mice with wings." But bats are insectivores, and mice are rodents. Bats have sharp teeth for seizing and eating insects and are more closely related to shrews than to mice.

Biggest Living Rodent

The capybara (*Hydrochoerus hydrochaeris*) of South America is the world's largest and heaviest rodent. Adults may be 4$\frac{1}{2}$ feet (1.4 m) long and weigh up to 175 pounds (79 kg), about as heavy as a truck tire, rim and all!

hy-drow-KEER-us hy-drow-KY-rus

This big, roly-poly rodent is also called the "water hog." It lives near water and can swim well, even diving beneath the water's surface to escape the jaguar, its worst enemy. When frightened, it can sprint faster than a person can run.

Ladybug

The smallest rodent is the northern pygmy mouse (*Baiomys taylori*). It lives in desert areas in Mexico, Texas, and Arizona. It may reach 4½ inches (11 cm) long, including its wispy little tail, and weighs only 0.28 ounce (8 g)—less than a dime.

Biggest Living Bird

You're grounded! When you think of birds, you usually think of creatures small and light enough to fly. But the biggest bird in the world, the ostrich, cannot fly. The ostrich (*Struthio camelus*) can be 9 feet (2.8 m) tall and weigh 340 pounds (150 kg), nearly as much as a refrigerator.

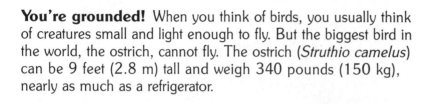

The 40-minute egg. The ostrich also lays the largest egg of all living birds. It is about 7 inches (18 cm) long and weighs almost 4 pounds (1.8 kg). Equal to about 20 hen's eggs, it takes about 40 minutes to hard-boil one!

 Ostrich

 Chicken

 Robin

 Hummingbird

Animal crackers. Ostriches lay their eggs on the ground, right out in the open. The eggs are so large and thick-shelled that even lions and hyenas cannot easily crack them. They often roll them around on the ground, unable to get a good grip. But the Egyptian vulture has learned to use a rock as a tool to break the eggs. The vulture is one of the few birds that use an object like a stone to accomplish a task it could not do otherwise.

STROOTH-ee-oh cam-ELL-us

Although the ostrich egg is the largest egg in the world, it is only about 1 percent of the mother ostrich's total weight.

Another flightless bird, the kiwi of New Zealand, is much smaller than the ostrich, but its egg may weigh more than a quarter of the mother's weight. The kiwi is about the size of a chicken, and its egg is nearly one-quarter the size of the ostrich's egg.

Marathon runners. The longer legs and fewer toes an animal has, the faster it can run. Grazing animals like antelopes have two toes and very long and slender legs so they can outrun predators. The ostrich is a grazing bird that lives in open country and it, too, has long legs and only two toes. It can run about 35 miles per hour, much faster than any other bird.

Biggest Flying Bird Ever

The largest flying bird that ever lived was the huge *Teratornis*, a vulture that looked something like the living California condor. The condor is a very big bird with a wingspan of 10 feet (3 m). Its great wings could spread out to 27 feet (8.2 m) —almost as wide as a small airplane!

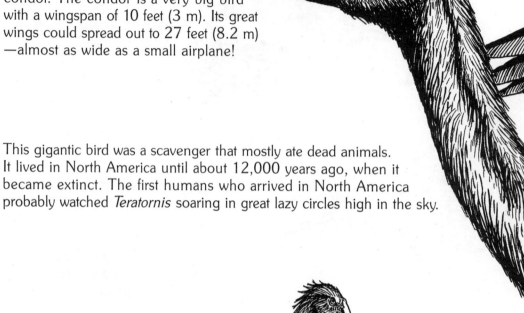

This gigantic bird was a scavenger that mostly ate dead animals. It lived in North America until about 12,000 years ago, when it became extinct. The first humans who arrived in North America probably watched *Teratornis* soaring in great lazy circles high in the sky.

Flightless birds, or "ratites," are almost always larger and heavier than birds that can fly. One of the biggest of all flightless birds was a moa called *Aepyornis*. It lived on the island of Madagascar millions of years ago. This huge bird stood 12 feet (3.8 m) tall and weighed about 1,000 pounds (450 kg), as much as a small pickup truck. Some moas survived until about 500 years ago, when they were finally killed by people.

terr-ah-TORN-uss ● AY-pee-OR-niss

Teratornis
condor

California
condor

Legs like an elephant.
Aepyornis had thick, strong
legs and was covered with
long feathers that looked like
hair. It has sometimes been
called the "elephant bird."

Biggest bird—biggest egg. The elephant bird also laid the biggest egg ever.
Paleontologists found one egg 33 inches (85 cm) long and 28 1/2 inches (72.3 cm)
around the middle. A fresh one would have weighed about 27 pounds (12.2 kg)—
eight times heavier than an ostrich egg—and could hold 2.35 gallons (8.88 liters).

Biggest Flying Animal Ever

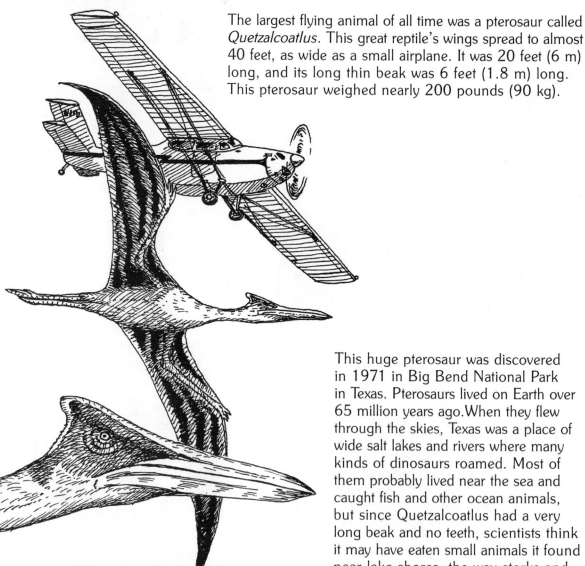

The largest flying animal of all time was a pterosaur called *Quetzalcoatlus*. This great reptile's wings spread to almost 40 feet, as wide as a small airplane. It was 20 feet (6 m) long, and its long thin beak was 6 feet (1.8 m) long. This pterosaur weighed nearly 200 pounds (90 kg).

This huge pterosaur was discovered in 1971 in Big Bend National Park in Texas. Pterosaurs lived on Earth over 65 million years ago. When they flew through the skies, Texas was a place of wide salt lakes and rivers where many kinds of dinosaurs roamed. Most of them probably lived near the sea and caught fish and other ocean animals, but since Quetzalcoatlus had a very long beak and no teeth, scientists think it may have eaten small animals it found near lake shores, the way storks and cranes do today. Scientists are still not sure how the quetzalcoatlus managed to raise its huge wings into the air. It may have lived on high cliffs near the sea so it could jump into the air and glide away.

kwet-zal-co-AT-lus

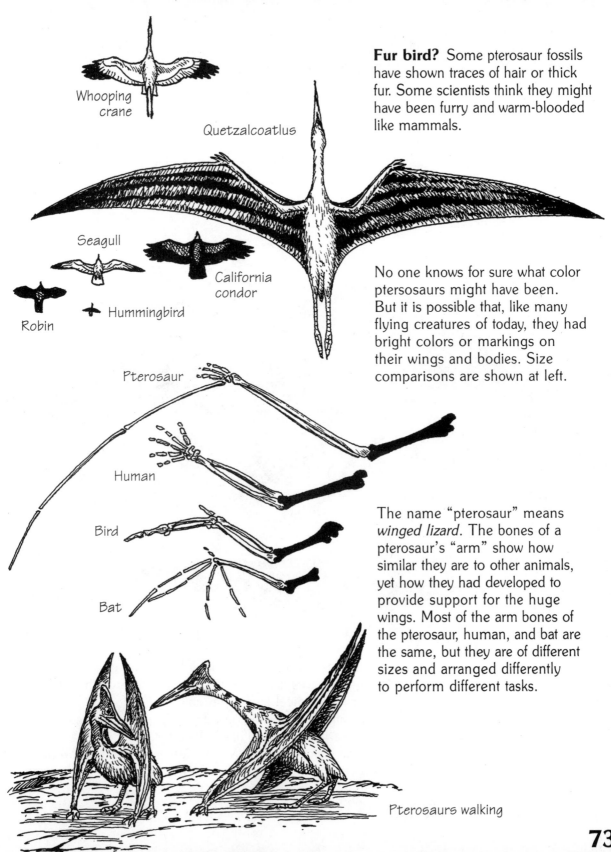

Whooping crane

Quetzalcoatlus

Fur bird? Some pterosaur fossils have shown traces of hair or thick fur. Some scientists think they might have been furry and warm-blooded like mammals.

Seagull

California condor

Robin

Hummingbird

No one knows for sure what color ptersosaurs might have been. But it is possible that, like many flying creatures of today, they had bright colors or markings on their wings and bodies. Size comparisons are shown at left.

Pterosaur

Human

Bird

Bat

The name "pterosaur" means *winged lizard*. The bones of a pterosaur's "arm" show how similar they are to other animals, yet how they had developed to provide support for the huge wings. Most of the arm bones of the pterosaur, human, and bat are the same, but they are of different sizes and arranged differently to perform different tasks.

Pterosaurs walking

73

Biggest Nest

The mallee fowl (*Leipoa ocellata*) of Australia, a bird related to chickens, builds the biggest nest of all birds. It lays its eggs in a pile of grasses and other plants that it collects from the forest. The pile may be 15 feet (4.6 m) high, 35 feet (11.2 m) across, and all of the plants in it may weigh more than 300 tons!

The mallee fowl is sometimes called the "incubator bird" because its nest—not the mother bird—warms, or incubates, its eggs. Leaves and grass become warm when they decay under the tropical sun. The male mallee fowl tests the temperature of the leaf pile with his beak, making sure that it is just warm enough to hatch the eggs. If the eggs are too cool, he covers them with more leaves. If they are too hot, he takes some of the plants off the nest.

LAY-poe-ah ah-sell-AT-ah

Compare the mallee fowl's enormous nest to the tiny nest of the world's smallest bird, the bee hummingbird. Its nest is the size of a sewing thimble and weighs about as much as a dust ball in the corner of a room!

Thimble

Big bird—big nest. The bald eagle of North America makes its nest in a tall tree. Usually a pair of eagles will add sticks and branches to it so that year after year it gets bigger and bigger. The largest eagle nest ever found was 12 feet (3.7 m) high, 11 feet (3.5 m) across. The tree it was in finally fell down and scientists weighed the nest material. It weighed 2 tons.

Longest Bill

The longest bird bill in the world belongs to the white pelican (*Pelecanus occidentalis*). It can be 20 inches (50 cm) long, and the pelican uses it as a scoop to catch the fish it eats.

pelly-CAN-uss ock-sih-DEN-tal-iss

The longest bird bill compared to the bird's body size belongs to the Andean sword-billed hummingbird (*Ensifera ensifera*) of South America. Its long slender bill is about 4 inches (10 cm) long, 1 inch longer than its 3-inch-long (7.5-cm) body. This hummer's bill is adapted to sipping nectar from very long flowers.

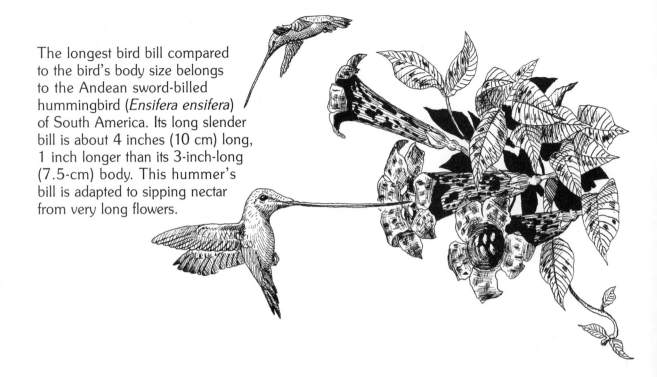

The longest known bird's tail does not belong to a wild bird, but to a domestic chicken, *Gallus gallus*. The Japanese onagodori rooster can have a tail 35 feet (11 m) long! It can grow 3 feet (1 m) per year. The roosters must spend most of their time sitting on a tall perch with the long tail carefully rolled up beneath them! Tails this long do not exist in wild birds. They would make getting around so difficult that the birds would soon be caught and eaten by predators.

Greatest Number of Feathers

All birds are covered with lots of feathers, but which birds have the most? One patient scientist who plucked and counted all the feathers from a tundra swan (*Cygnus columbianus*) discovered that the bird had 25,216 feathers, more than any other bird. Most of the feathers—20,177 of them—were on the bird's head and long neck.

SIGG-nuss ko-lumm-bee-ANN-uss

One tiny ruby-throated hummingbird (*Archilochus colubris*) had 940 feathers on its wings and body. That's more feathers per body area than any other bird.

Earliest Bird

For a long time scientists have suspected that birds are descended from dinosaurs, and now they're almost sure of it. A small dinosaur with some bones closely resembling those of modern birds has been discovered in Argentina. The paleontologist who found the little dino named it *Unenlagia comahuensis*. Its name means "half bird from northwest Patagonia" in the language of the Indians who live there.

The dinosaur connection. *Unenlagia* lived about 90 million years ago, when there were dinosaurs on the Earth. It was about 4 feet (1.2 m) tall and 7 feet (2.2 m) long and ran on its hind legs, like a little tyrannosaur. The shoulder and arm bones of this little dinosaur show that it could probably flap its forelegs up and down, like a bird does with its wings, but that it could not actually fly.

oo-nen-LAH-gee-ah kom-ah-hoo-ENN-sis

The first "real" bird. A small creature called *Archaeopteryx* is believed to be another ancestor of birds. It lived about 145 million years ago, long before *Unenlagia* was alive. Seven skeletons of *Archaeopteryx* have been found. They show that this crow-sized animal had true feathers like our modern birds and that it could fly. It also had a long bony tail, like dinosaurs did. This early bird's name means "ancient wing."

Archaeopteryx fossil found in Germany

Longest Wingspan

The wandering albatross (*Diomedea exulans*) is the flying bird with the longest wingspan. When its long, narrow wings are open, they spread to nearly 11 feet (3.5 m) wider than any other bird. The albatross can glide for as much as 100 miles (160 km) over the sea without flapping its wings once. In fact, the albatross needs to be near land only to lay its eggs and raise its young. It spends about 90 percent of its entire life on the wing.

The albatross may be a very big bird, but it is not heavy. It weighs only about 15 pounds (6.8 kg). By contrast, some flying birds, such as swans or turkeys, weigh 25 or 30 pounds (14 kg). But *really* heavy birds like ostriches can't fly at all. For a 300-pound (138 kg) ostrich to fly, it would have to have a wingspread of at least 30 feet (9 m)!

Prepare for takeoff!
Albatrosses can't just jump into the air and fly away as most small birds can. When the albatross wants to take off, it opens up its great wings, runs into the wind, and just lifts off into the sky.

dye-oh-MEED-ah EX-oo-lans

Warm and cozy. An albatross's feathers do a lot more than help it fly. They also protect the bird against the cold and winds of its island home. Feathers also make it more streamlined and, because they are so light, they keep the bird's weight down.

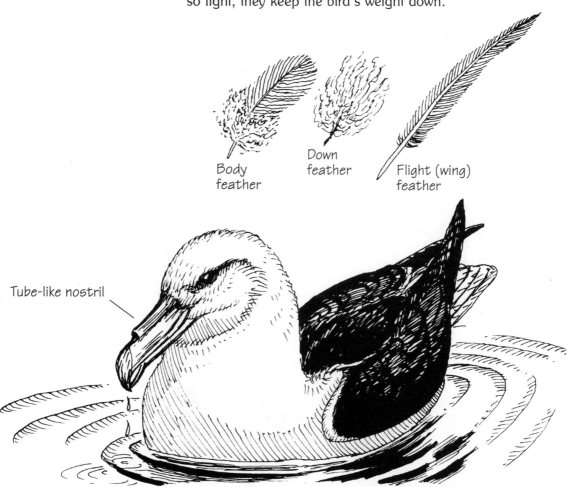

Body feather

Down feather

Flight (wing) feather

Tube-like nostril

Pass the salt. Albatrosses and their relatives, called *shearwaters*, are among the few animals that can safely drink salt water. They have special glands that get rid of the excess salt in their bodies. The birds shake the crusty salt out through the tube-like nostrils on their bills.

Biggest Living Butterfly

Insects in warm parts of the world usually grow larger and have brighter colors than their more northern relatives. The birdwing butterfly (*Ornithoptera alexandrae*) lives on a few islands in the South Pacific Ocean and is the world's largest butterfly. Its wings, spread out, measure 12 inches (30 cm) across. This is about as wide as a pigeon's wings and 6 times wider than most of our own common butterflies.

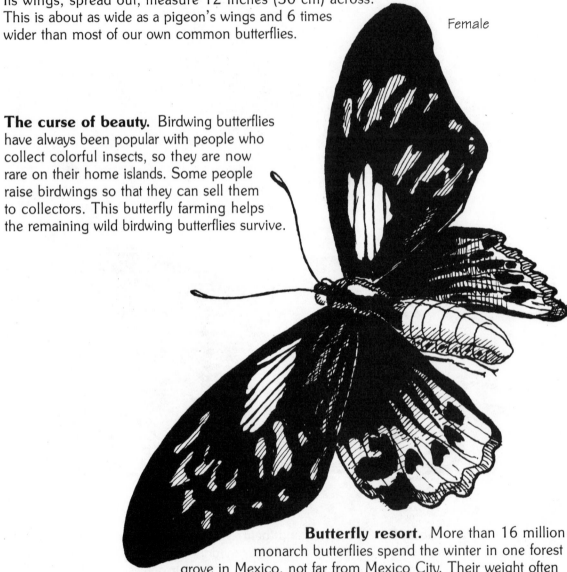

Female

The curse of beauty. Birdwing butterflies have always been popular with people who collect colorful insects, so they are now rare on their home islands. Some people raise birdwings so that they can sell them to collectors. This butterfly farming helps the remaining wild birdwing butterflies survive.

Butterfly resort. More than 16 million monarch butterflies spend the winter in one forest grove in Mexico, not far from Mexico City. Their weight often makes the tree branches sag to the ground. One town in California where monarchs gather for the winter calls itself "Butterfly Town USA." People who bother the butterflies there risk a stiff fine and even jail.

orr-nith-OPP-terr-ah alex-ANN-dray

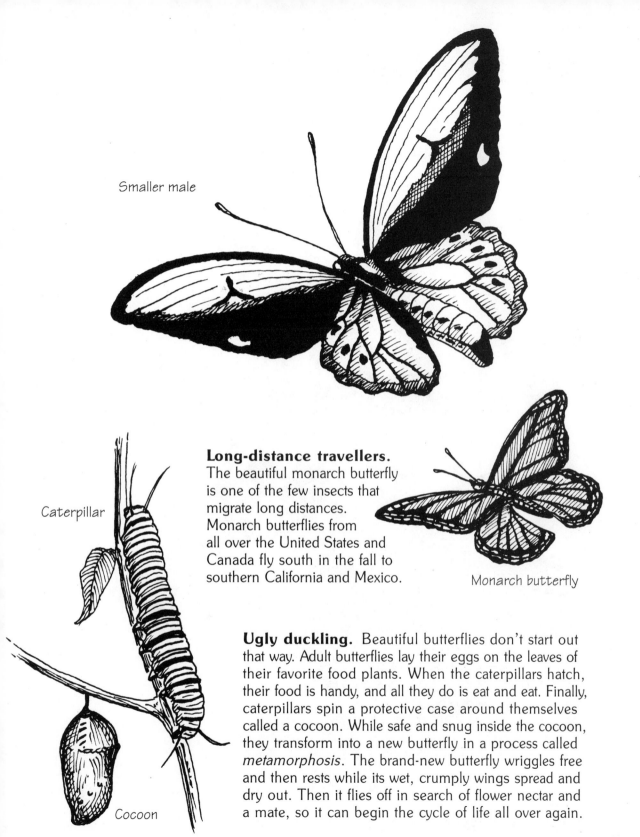

Smaller male

Caterpillar

Cocoon

Long-distance travellers.
The beautiful monarch butterfly
is one of the few insects that
migrate long distances.
Monarch butterflies from
all over the United States and
Canada fly south in the fall to
southern California and Mexico.

Monarch butterfly

Ugly duckling. Beautiful butterflies don't start out
that way. Adult butterflies lay their eggs on the leaves of
their favorite food plants. When the caterpillars hatch,
their food is handy, and all they do is eat and eat. Finally,
caterpillars spin a protective case around themselves
called a cocoon. While safe and snug inside the cocoon,
they transform into a new butterfly in a process called
metamorphosis. The brand-new butterfly wriggles free
and then rests while its wet, crumply wings spread and
dry out. Then it flies off in search of flower nectar and
a mate, so it can begin the cycle of life all over again.

Heaviest Living Insect

The Goliath beetle (*Goliath goliathus*) of Africa is the heaviest known insect in the world. It is 5 inches (12 cm) long and weighs about a quarter of a pound (4 oz or 90 g). That may not sound heavy, but it is as much as a quarter-pounder hamburger! Most of the world's insects weigh less than a quarter-ounce each.

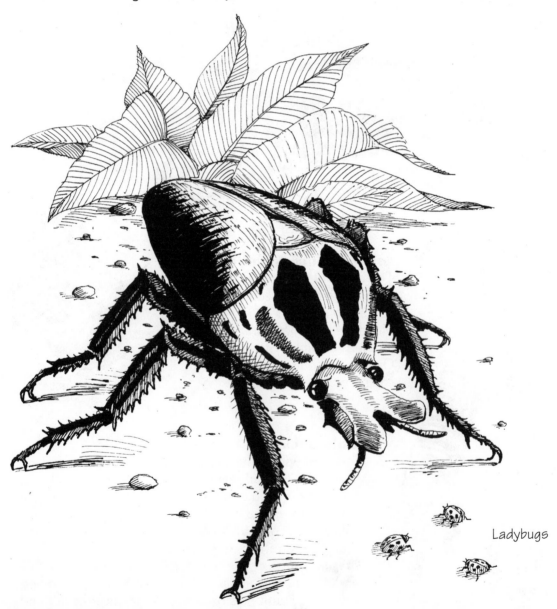

Ladybugs

go-LYE-ath go-LYE-ath-uss

Goliath beetles look scary and frighten people because they are so large. But they are harmless—to people, anyway. They eat the sap and buds of palm trees, which stops the trees from growing. But this isn't a big problem because Goliath beetles are not abundant where palm trees grow.

The Goliath beetle is named after a soldier in the Bible who was 7 feet (2.2 m) tall and very strong. The beetle is also the strongest insect in the world. It can grip a branch so powerfully that monkeys and even people cannot pull them off. In a test, scientists found that the beetle could support 850 times its own weight. The strongest humans can support or hold only 17 times their own weight.

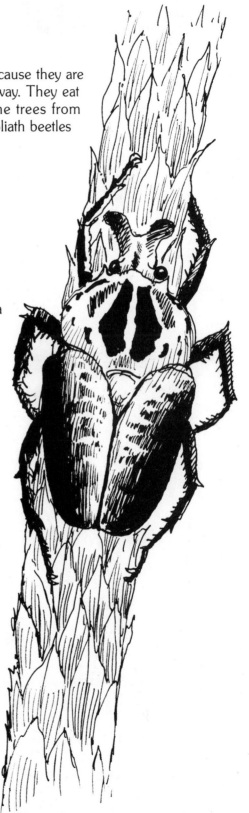

Longest Living Insect

The longest living insect is a stick insect (*Pharnacia serratipes*) that lives in the jungles of Borneo. Its body can be 13 inches (32 cm) long, that's almost twice as long as an ordinary pencil. Including its legs, it may be more than 20 inches (50 cm) long.

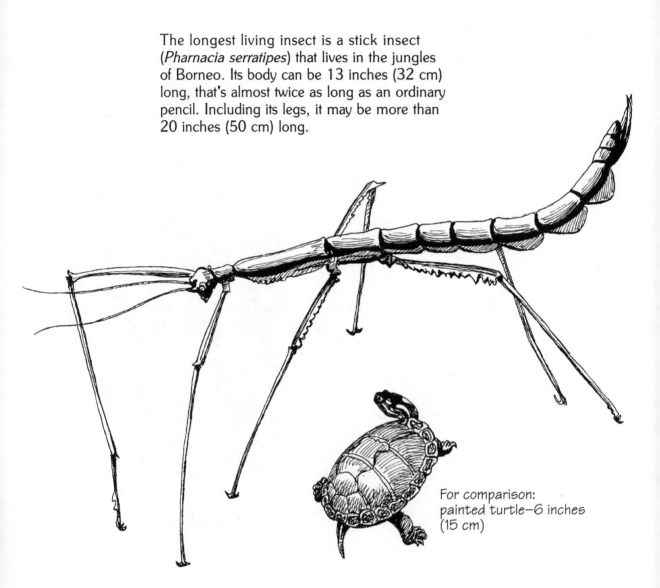

For comparison: painted turtle—6 inches (15 cm)

far-NAY-see-ya serr-ah-TIH-pees

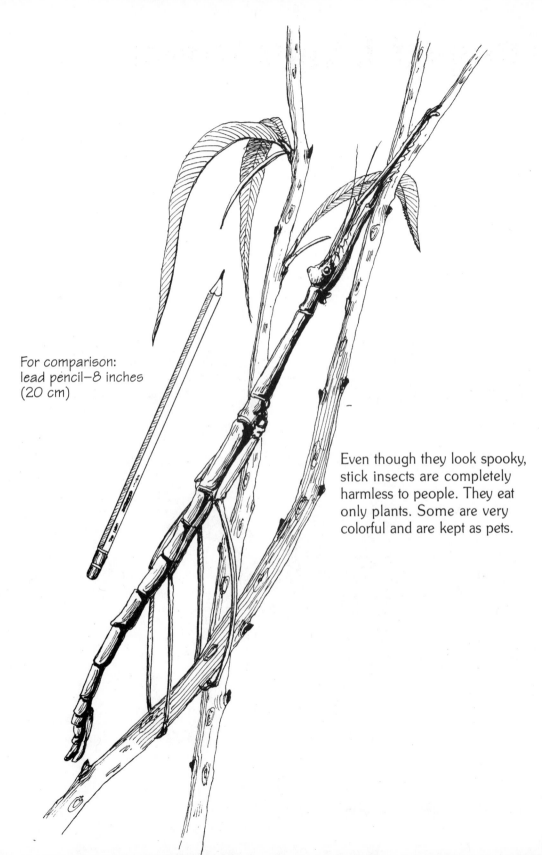

For comparison:
lead pencil—8 inches
(20 cm)

Even though they look spooky,
stick insects are completely
harmless to people. They eat
only plants. Some are very
colorful and are kept as pets.

Biggest Insect Ever

The biggest insect in the world, as far as we know, was *Meganeura*, a giant dragonfly that lived about 220 million years ago. Its wings spread to 28 inches (70 cm), about as wide as a crow's wings. Meganeura lived during the Carboniferous Period, when great forests of giant ferns covered much of our planet.

megg-ah-NOO-rah

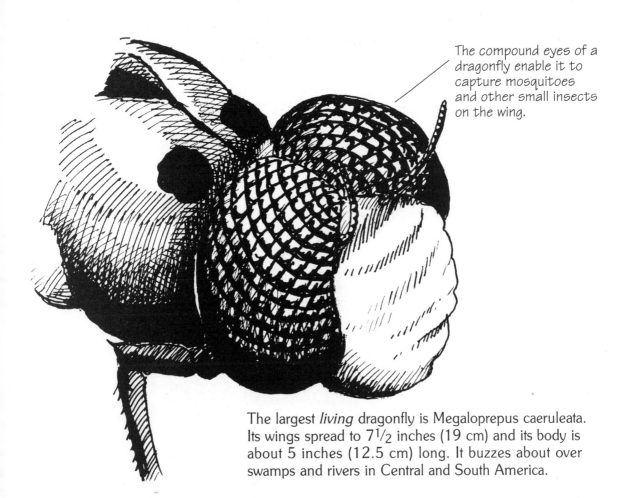

The compound eyes of a dragonfly enable it to capture mosquitoes and other small insects on the wing.

The largest *living* dragonfly is Megaloprepus caeruleata. Its wings spread to $7\frac{1}{2}$ inches (19 cm) and its body is about 5 inches (12.5 cm) long. It buzzes about over swamps and rivers in Central and South America.

Dragonfly laying eggs in water

Dragonfly facts.
All dragonflies are swift,
expert fliers with good eyesight.
They can easily snatch small insects out of the air.
Female dragonflies lay their eggs in water one at a time by
flitting just above the water's surface and depositing each egg while flying.

Longest Earthworm

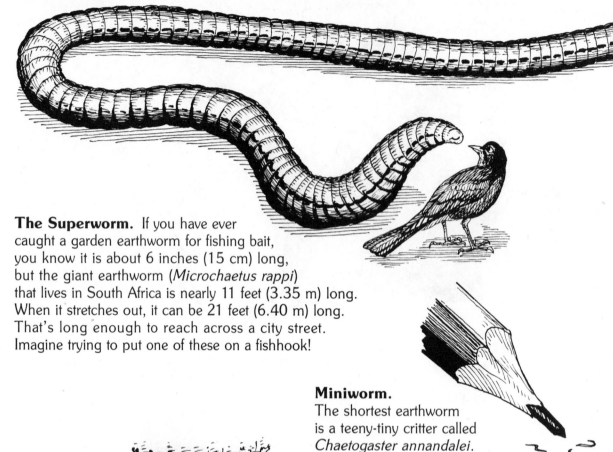

The Superworm. If you have ever caught a garden earthworm for fishing bait, you know it is about 6 inches (15 cm) long, but the giant earthworm (*Microchaetus rappi*) that lives in South Africa is nearly 11 feet (3.35 m) long. When it stretches out, it can be 21 feet (6.40 m) long. That's long enough to reach across a city street. Imagine trying to put one of these on a fishhook!

Miniworm. The shortest earthworm is a teeny-tiny critter called *Chaetogaster annandalei*. It is 0.019 inch (0.5 mm) long, about one-quarter the length of a grain of rice.

High and dry. Earthworms often climb trees, mostly to get away from water. Some have been found 20 feet (6 m) up in trees, hiding beneath the bark. When the weather is too dry, earthworms may burrow underground as far as 8 feet (2.5 m).

mike-roh-KEE-tuss rapp-eye

Nature's gardeners.
Earthworms help keep soil healthy by tunnelling so that air is circulated underground. They also eat leaves and other plants and add them to the soil. Without earthworms, the soil would soon become hard and lifeless. Scientists estimate that there may be as many as 3 million earthworms per acre in grassy areas.

Brainy worms? Earthworms don't have eyes, but are they brainless, too? Scientists have watched worms pulling leaves down into their burrows. A leaf is much easier to pull into a hole by its end rather than by its edge. The worms grabbed a leaf and tugged on it. They tried again and again until they grabbed the leaf's stem or tip. Then the leaf slipped down the hole easily. Was it luck, or did they actually figure it out?

Biggest Appetite for Its Weight

The Great Gulper! The caterpillar of the polyphemus moth (*Antheraea polyphemus*) is the record-holder for the amount of food eaten compared to weight. The polyphemus caterpillar, or larva, can eat so many plant leaves that they amount to 86,000 times its weight as it emerges from its cocoon. And it does this in the first 48 hours of its life!

To equal the polyphemus caterpillar's eating record, a human baby weighing 7 pounds (3.2 kg) would have to eat 273 *tons* of baby food in the same period of time!

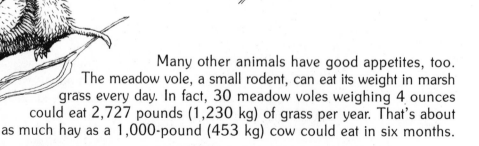

Many other animals have good appetites, too. The meadow vole, a small rodent, can eat its weight in marsh grass every day. In fact, 30 meadow voles weighing 4 ounces could eat 2,727 pounds (1,230 kg) of grass per year. That's about as much hay as a 1,000-pound (453 kg) cow could eat in six months.

ann-ther-AY-ah polly-FEE-muss

94

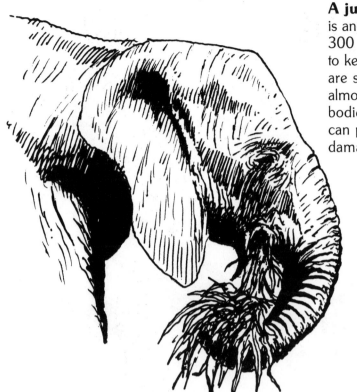

A jumbo appetite. The elephant is another big eater. It needs about 300 pounds (135 kg) of food a day to keep in shape. In fact, elephants are so large that they must eat almost constantly to fuel their huge bodies. A large herd of elephants can pull down trees and severely damage a forest in a week or two.

Fast food. Lions need about 15 pounds (7.5 kg) of meat a day. But lions, as well as most mammal predators, may eat a lot of food all at once when they can get it and then spend a day or two snoozing and resting up for the next hunt.

Biggest Living Spider

Did you ever hear of a spider big enough to catch and eat a small bird or lizard? The Goliath bird spider (*Theraphosa leblondi*) of South America, which is related to the tarantula spiders, is the largest spider in the world. Its body is 3½ inches (9 cm) long, and its legs spread across 11 inches (27.5 cm)—wider than a baseball cap.

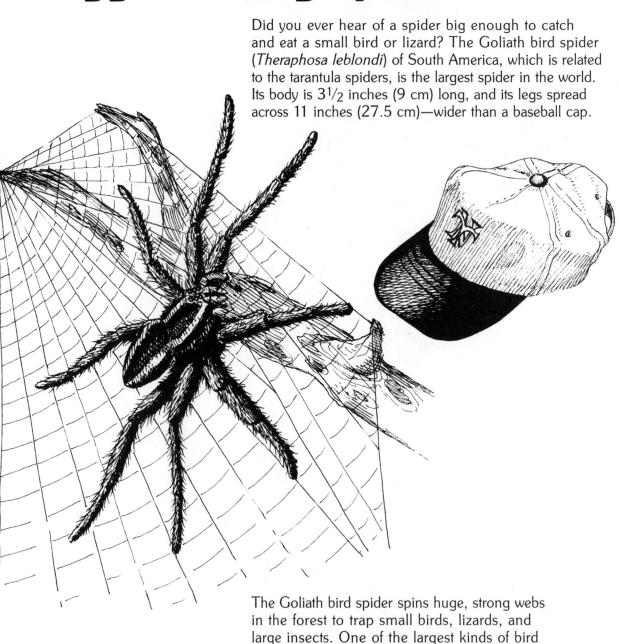

The Goliath bird spider spins huge, strong webs in the forest to trap small birds, lizards, and large insects. One of the largest kinds of bird spiders lives in Brazil. It often catches and eats frogs, lizards, and even poisonous snakes, even though it may take a day to eat its prey.

ther-ah-FO-sah lee-BLON-dye

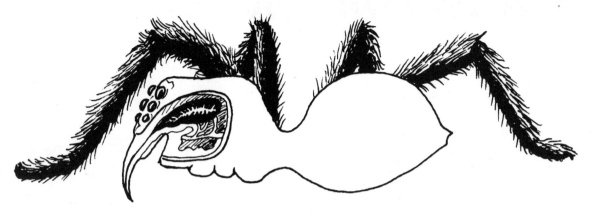

Bird spiders can live for more than 25 years. (By contrast, most pet dogs live only about 15 years.) Most spiders have poison, or venom, which they use to kill their prey, but the amount injected by the bite of most species is so small that it is not dangerous to people.

While few people would think of a bird spider as a pet, the similar red-legged tarantula of Mexico is in fact a very popular pet. Tarantulas look dangerous and they can bite, but they have easy-going "personalities" (for spiders) and quickly get used to people. Spider owners often handle their pets—but carefully!

Most Electric Fish

A few kinds of fishes deliver electric shocks as part of their defense against predators. The fish with the most powerful electrical system is the electric eel (*Electrophorus electricus*) of South America. This fish can deliver an electric shock of 400 volts. Some eel shocks have been measured at 650 volts—strong enough to knock down a horse. Electric eels have more than enough "juice" to light up dozens of light bulbs.

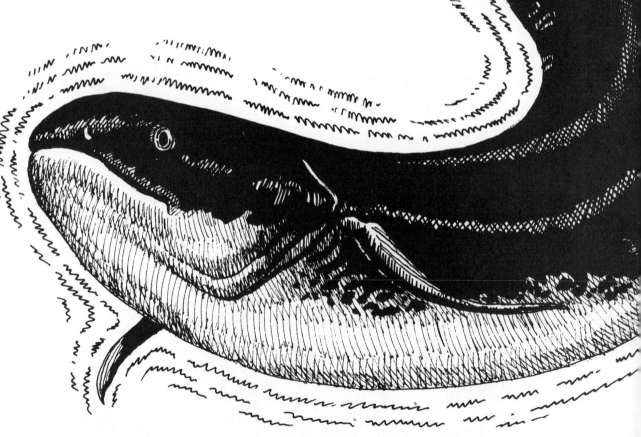

EE-leck-trow-FOR-uss EE-leck-trih-kuss

The electric catfish
(*Malapterus electricus*) is smaller
than the electric eel, but it can deliver
a pretty strong shock, too. Small ones
can produce about 60 volts when disturbed,
enough to make your hand and arm numb.

The electric eel and electric catfish produce strong
shocks only when they are attacked. Usually, they generate
much milder electric pulses that help them locate prey or
find their way about in the murky jungle waters where they live.

Heaviest Living Snake

The largest living snake in the world is the anaconda, or water boa (*Eunectes murinus*), of South America. These big snakes usually live near water, and the largest measured was 37 feet (11.4 m) long, almost as long as a city bus. It weighed 1,100 pounds (498 kg)! Most anacondas are smaller—about 25 feet (7.3 m) long and 500 pounds (227 kg). But even one this size could kill and eat a small deer or pig.

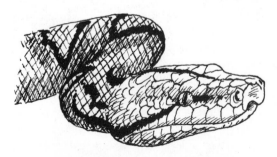

The reticulated python, *Python reticulatus*, of Southeast Asia and Indonesia can also get pretty big. Some have been measured at almost 33 feet (10.2 m) long, and there may be even longer ones in the jungles.

you-NECK-tees mure-EE-nus

The biggest snake ever was a giant python that lived in Africa about 55 million years ago. This snake, *Gigantophis garstini*, was about 38 feet (11.8 m) long. Scientists have found only parts of its backbone, but they were able to estimate its size from of the size of these bones, or vertebrae.

Pythons and boas don't kill their prey by wrapping themselves around it and crushing its bones. They squeeze, or constrict, tighter and tighter until the prey cannot breathe. The bones of a snake's jaws are loosely connected so that they can unhinge from the skull. This allows the snake to swallow very large prey.

Drawing showing how the snake's lower jaw spreads

Gigantophis garstini

Many stories about pythons and anacondas eating people have been told, but only a few of them have been proven. Most big snakes avoid people whenever they can because humans are much more dangerous to snakes than the snakes are to them.

Most Poisonous Living Snake

The most poisonous snake in the world is *Hydrophis belcheri*.
It lives in the Timor Sea in Southeast Asia. This sea snake's
venom is 100 times more toxic than that of the king cobra of
India, one of the most poisonous land snakes in the world.
Even though it has the strongest poison of any snake, very
few people have died from the bite of a sea snake.
This is because it is an easy-going creature that
seldom bites, even when handled by divers.

Sea snake tails are flattened like paddles to help them move through
the water. Most sea snakes never come ashore because they are
helpless on land. They do not lay eggs like most snakes do, but
give birth to living young at sea.

hi-DROW-fiss BELL-cherr-eye

The *longest* poisonous snake is the king cobra, *Ophiophagus hannah*, of India and Malaysia. These aggressive snakes average 12 to 15 feet (3.6–4.5 m) long. The longest one ever measured was 18 feet, 2 inches (5.5 m) long when it was caught, and it grew another 7 inches (18 cm) while it lived at a zoo.

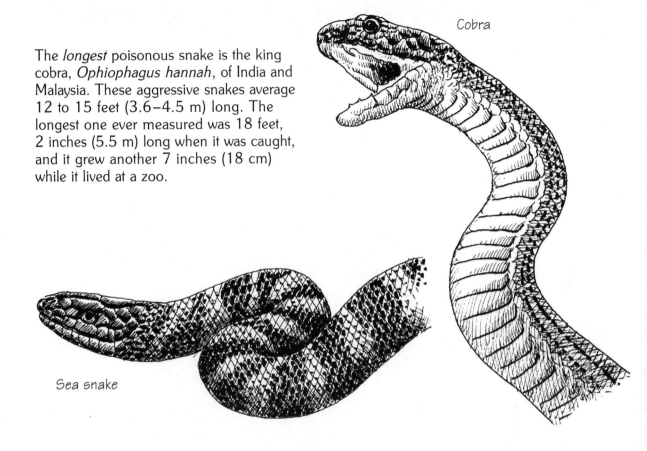

Cobra

Sea snake

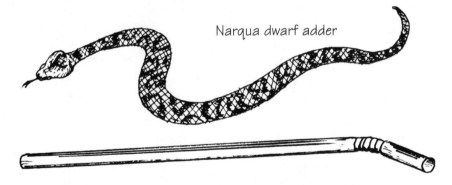

Narqua dwarf adder

The shortest poisonous snake is the Narqua dwarf adder (*Bitis schneideri*) of Namibia, Africa. A big one is about 8 inches (20 cm) long, as long as a drinking straw.

Most Poisonous Living Animal

The tiny, brightly colored arrow poison frogs of Central and South America carry the strongest poison of all frogs. Their poison is so powerful that it can kill a human or a large animal in less than an hour.

The most poisonous of the arrow poison frogs is the golden arrow poison frog (*Phyllobates terribilis*). This tiny creature is only about 2 inches (5 cm) long, but scientists handling it always wear thick gloves. South American Indian tribes use the poison taken from these frogs on the tips of their arrows to hunt monkeys and other animals.

fye-low-BAY-tees terr-ih-BILL-iss

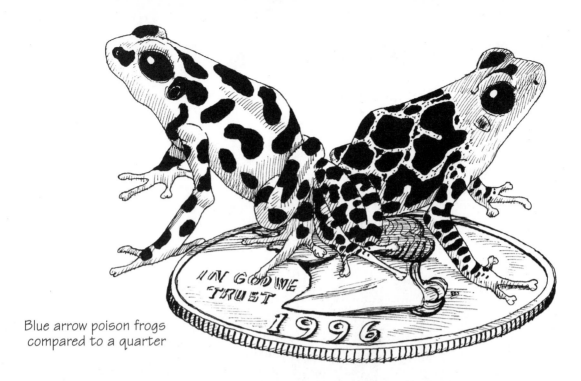

Blue arrow poison frogs
compared to a quarter

Pretty poison. While most wild creatures have colors that blend into their habitats and help them hide from predators, many poisonous animals are brightly colored. They can be easily spotted among plants and often move about boldly because most predators recognize that the creature's bright colors are a warning.

In some species of arrow poison frogs the male carries the tiny tadpoles on his back until they can fend for themselves.

Only Snake with Legs

One of the "sure things" that make a snake a snake is "no legs." Although some boas and pythons alive today have tiny leg bones embedded in their bodies, no living snakes have actual legs. But scientists recently decided that a lizard fossil found 20 years ago was a snake—and that this snake had legs. They named it *Pachyrachis problematicus*.

The first sea snake? This 36-inch-long (75-cm) primitive snake lived about 95 million years ago in what is today Israel. In the Age of Reptiles, that area was a warm, shallow sea. So *Pachyrachis* was probably a good swimmer and similar to our modern sea snakes.

Pachyrachis had two small (1 inch or 2.5 cm) strong hind legs but no front legs. When this fossil snake was first discovered, paleontologists thought it was a lizard simply because it had legs—even if there were only two.

packy-RACK-iss prob-lem-AT-ih-kuss

A real "problematicus."

Part of this snake's scientific name means "problem" or "puzzle." This is because scientists are still not sure just how snakes evolved and lost their legs. Some think snakes developed from ground-burrowing lizards, while others believe they are descended from the giant marine lizards called mosasaurs.

Mosasaur

Lizard

Snake

Legless lizard

Lizards without legs. Some lizards that burrow in the soil have no legs and look a lot like snakes. An easy way to tell them from snakes is that lizard eyes always have eyelids and snakes do not. Legless lizards are sometimes called "glass snakes" or "worm lizards."

Biggest Living Crab

King crab. Did you know that the world's largest crab could stand over a sports car and there would still be room for the roof rack? The giant spider crab (*Machrocheira kaempferi*) lives in deep, cold water off the coast of Japan. Its body is only about 14 inches (35 cm) wide, but its legs can span up to 18 feet (5.5 m). One crab that had a claw span of 12 feet (3.6 m) weighed 41 pounds (18.6 kg). That's a lot of crab salad!

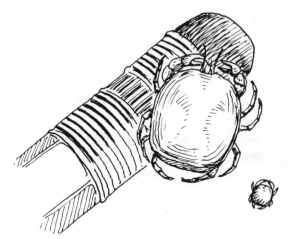

The peewee pea crab. What about the smallest crab in the world? These are the "pea crabs" that live in cool seas near the British Isles. The smallest pea crab is *Pinotheres pisum*, a tiny creature whose back shell, or carapace, is only 1/4-inch wide (6.3 mm).

Pea crab (actual size)

mack-ro-KEE-ra CAM-fer-eye

A lobster lunker. Crabs are crustaceans, which means that their hard skeleton is on the outside rather than the inside of their bodies. The giant spider crab is the *largest*, but not the *heaviest* of all crustaceans. That honor belongs to the North American lobster (*Homarus americanus*). One lobster that was caught near Nova Scotia, Canada, weighed 45 pounds (20 kg). This lobster was 3 feet, 6 inches (1.06 m) long from the tip of its largest claw to the end of its tail. It was eventually sold to a restaurant, where it was displayed to the public.

For comparison:
a one-pound (454-g) lobster

A little freeloader. Pea crabs are parasites that live inside live clams or mussels. They mooch off the clams and mussels by eating some of the food that the bivalves (meaning "two shells") strain from the water for themselves.

Seahorse, mollusks, and pea crabs

Biggest Living Starfish

There are 1,600 different kinds of starfish in the world, most of them rather small. But the long, thin arms of a brittle star (*Midgardia xandaros*), of the Gulf of Mexico may reach 54 inches (135 cm) across. Even though this brittle star is the world's largest starfish, its tiny body is only a little wider than a quarter (25 mm).

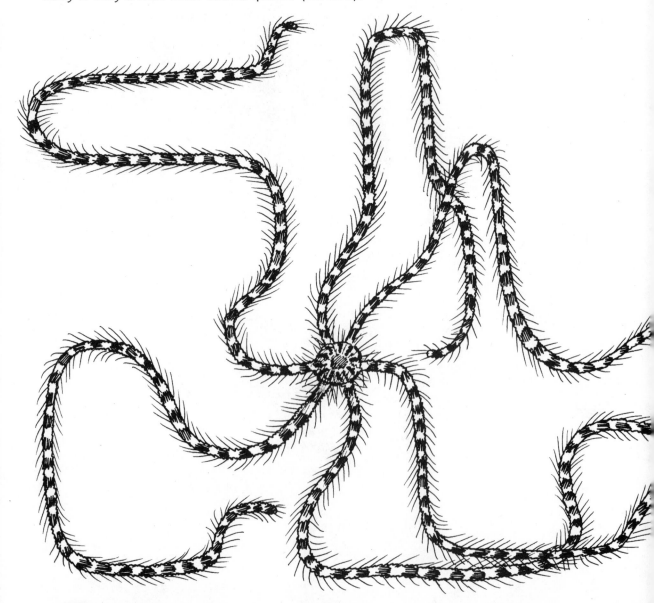

mid-GAR-dee-tah zan-DAR-oss

The heaviest known starfish is *Thromidia catalai* of the western Pacific Ocean. The heaviest one ever found weighed 13 pounds (6 kg)—more than a house cat. This big seastar has five arms, and they may spread to 25 inches (62 cm).

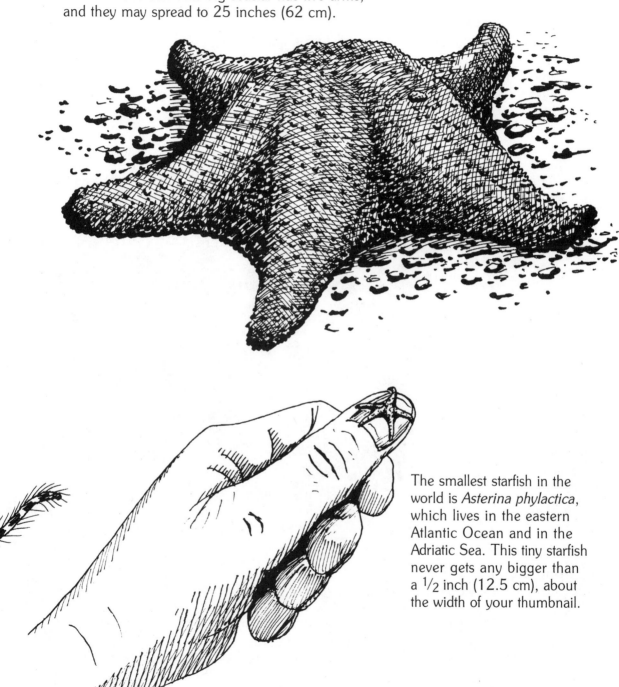

The smallest starfish in the world is *Asterina phylactica*, which lives in the eastern Atlantic Ocean and in the Adriatic Sea. This tiny starfish never gets any bigger than a 1/2 inch (12.5 cm), about the width of your thumbnail.

Biggest Seashell

The largest sea shell in the world comes from the giant clam (*Tridacna*) of the tropical Pacific Ocean. Its great shells can be up to 5 feet (1.5 m) across, and the living clam can weigh 580 pounds (263 kg). The 5- to 7-inch (12–18 cm)-wide pearls that this clam produces can weigh up to 15 pounds (7 kg) each. Not the size you might use for a necklace!

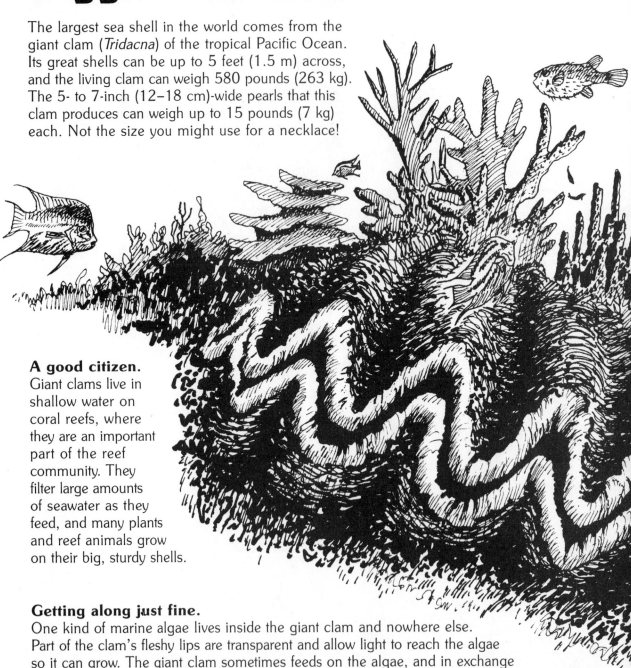

A good citizen.
Giant clams live in shallow water on coral reefs, where they are an important part of the reef community. They filter large amounts of seawater as they feed, and many plants and reef animals grow on their big, sturdy shells.

Getting along just fine.
One kind of marine algae lives inside the giant clam and nowhere else. Part of the clam's fleshy lips are transparent and allow light to reach the algae so it can grow. The giant clam sometimes feeds on the algae, and in exchange the algae gets the protection of the huge clam's thick tank-like shells. This kind of cooperative arrangement is called *symbiosis*, which means "living together."

try-DACK-nah

Diver beware! Old movies about the sea often show divers getting caught by the hand or foot and drowned by giant clams, but there is no proof that this has ever actually happened. The clam is so large and heavy that its valves close too slowly to trap a swimmer or diver.

The not-so-happy-as-a-clam. Really big giant clams are not as common as they once were. Large numbers have died when reefs have been damaged by pollution or muddy water coming off nearby land. Others have been collected for food. Smaller clams are often taken from reefs for marine aquariums. The shells of the big ones are often cleaned and used for home decorations, birdbaths, or even bathtubs for people! Because they are becoming rare, giant clams are now raised on special clam farms in shallow tropical waters.

Biggest Living Toad

A load of toad. The biggest toad in the world is the marine toad (*Bufo marinus*). The biggest one ever caught was about $9\frac{1}{2}$ inches (23.8 cm) long and weighed in at nearly 3 pounds (1.2 kg). That's about as heavy as a full-grown pet rabbit.

Lubber grasshopper (2 inches or 5 cm)

American toad

An unwelcome immigrant. The marine toad has been transported all over the tropical world to help control insect pests, but sometimes it becomes a pest itself. Some were brought to Australia about 25 years ago to eat crop-eating insects. Today, millions of toads overrun gardens and towns in many areas. They eat both good and bad insects and even help themselves to bowls of dog and cat food left outside!

BOO-fo mar-EE-nuss

A bite-sized *Bufo*. The smallest toad in the world is *Bufo taitanus beiranus*, a tiny creature living in Africa. This toad reaches only 0.94 inch (24 mm) when it is full-grown. Although it is a tiny toad, *Bufo beiranus* has the same type of poison glands as the huge marine toad, to protect it from predators.

For comparison: smallest toad and ordinary pencil head

Look but don't eat! All *Bufo* toads have a strong poison in special glands on their heads. The poison is not harmful to people's skin and will not give you warts, as many people believe. But other animals—a dog or cat, even a skunk—can become very sick if it grabs a toad in its mouth. A North American snake called the hognose snake dines on toads and is not bothered by its poison.

115

Biggest Living Frog

Most of the world's frogs average about 3½ inches (9 cm) from snout to rump, but one frog gets much larger. It's the Goliath frog (*Rana goliath*) of Africa. One large female measured 32 inches (80 cm) long with her legs stretched out. She weighed 7 pounds, 4 ounces (0.1 kg). Compare this to North America's largest frog, the bullfrog, which is about 7 inches (18 cm) from snout to rump.

American bullfrog

RAN-nah go-LIE-ath

116

For comparison: showing an adult guinea pig—11 inches (28 cm)

Biggest Living Salamander

The Pacific giant salamander *Dicamplodon ensatus* reaches 6 inches (15 cm) in length and is one of the largest salamanders in North America. But it is a real pygmy when compared to the record-holding Chinese giant salamander (*Andrias davidianus*), which averages 3 feet, 10 inches (1.2 m) long and can weigh up to 65 pounds (30 kg). One was 5 feet, 11 inches (1.8 m) long and weighed 143 pounds (65 kg), as much as a full-grown Rottweiler dog!

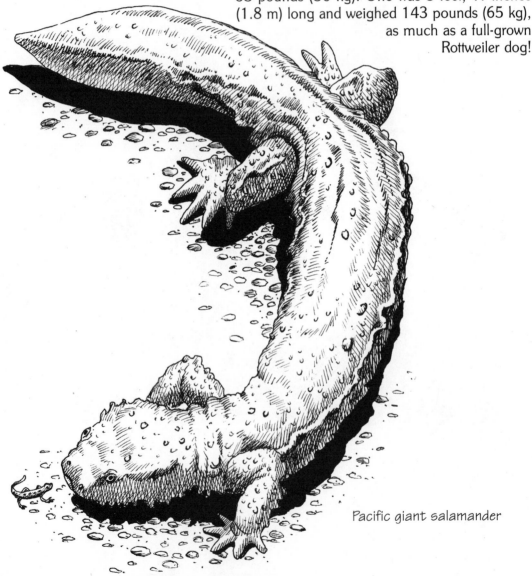

Pacific giant salamander

ann-DRY-ass dav-id-ee-ANN-us

The second largest salamander in the world is the Japanese giant salamander (*Andrias japonicus*). It often reaches 5 feet (1.5 m) long and can weigh up to 88 pounds (40 kg). This salamander also holds the record for longevity among amphibians. One lived for 55 years at the Amsterdam Zoo.

Both the Chinese and Japanese giant salamanders live in cold mountain streams and marshes, where they hunt fishes at night. You may never have tasted one, but salamanders are good to eat, and the Japanese giant salamander has been hunted for food so much that it is now an endangered species.

Japanese giant salamander

Biggest Living Flower

A lollapalooza of a lily.
The world's largest flower
is on a plant called the
corpse lily (*Rafflesia arnoldi*).
It lives as a parasite only on
certain vines in the dense
rain forests of Southeast Asia.

Real stinker.
The corpse lily gets its name because
it smells like rotten meat, when it blooms.
The huge flower can be 3 feet (1 m) across and
weigh up to 15 pounds (7 kg). Each petal looks like a big piece
of leather often 3/4-inch (2 cm) thick. Not an easy flower to pick!

Venus flytrap leaf

The attack of the killer plants!
Most plants take their nourishment from rain,
soil, air, and sunlight. A few, though, have to
work a little harder for their food. These are
the carnivorous, or meat-eating plants.

raff-LESS-ee-ya arr-NOLD-eye

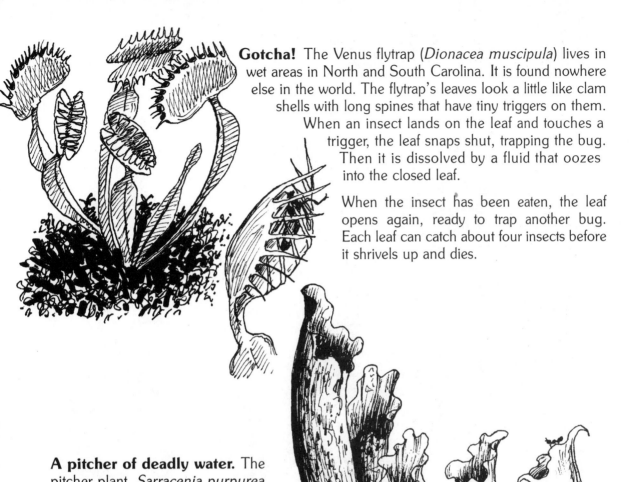

Gotcha! The Venus flytrap (*Dionacea muscipula*) lives in wet areas in North and South Carolina. It is found nowhere else in the world. The flytrap's leaves look a little like clam shells with long spines that have tiny triggers on them. When an insect lands on the leaf and touches a trigger, the leaf snaps shut, trapping the bug. Then it is dissolved by a fluid that oozes into the closed leaf.

When the insect has been eaten, the leaf opens again, ready to trap another bug. Each leaf can catch about four insects before it shrivels up and dies.

A pitcher of deadly water. The pitcher plant, *Sarracenia purpurea*, grows in wet bogs. It has hollow, tubelike leaves lined with downward-pointing hairs, and water collects in the bottom of the tube. The plants produce a sweet substance that attracts insects, which fall into the trap and cannot climb back out. Then they fall into the water and drown. The pitcher plant then dissolves and digests their bodies.

A sticky situation. The sun dew, *Drosera rotundifolia*, has tiny leaves covered with tiny hairs. Each hair has a sticky, shiny droplet on the end. Any insect that lands on the leaves gets stuck in the droplets. When that happens, the leaf curls around the bug and the plant digests it. When only the insect's hard parts are left, the leaf opens up again.

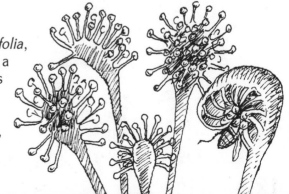

Biggest Seed

If you have ever helped plant a garden, you have noticed how small many of the seeds are. But there is one seed that can weigh 40 pounds (18 kg) and is larger than a basketball. It is the seed of a certain palm tree that grows on the Seychelle Islands in the Indian Ocean and is called a double coconut (*Lodoicea seychellarum*).

Turning a new leaf. The double coconut is actually the seed of the raffia palm, which also has the world's largest leaves. All palm trees live in warmer climates, usually near the sea. Their leaves are used to make baskets, thatch roofs for houses, and even lawn furniture.

Long-distance travelers. Palm trees can spread across the sea to other islands. Their coconuts often fall from the tree into water and float for hundreds of miles before reaching land. When the waves toss them up on a beach, the coconut sends roots down into the sand and a new palm tree sprouts.

low-DOY-see-ya say-shell-AR-um

Humongous leaves.

Raffia palm leaves can be over 60 feet (19 m) long, as high as a 6-story building. The leaves and trunk fibers of the raffia palm are used for tying plants and making baskets and hats.

Palm leaf

Most palm leaves are made up of many smaller "leaflets," so they are not really one leaf. The biggest *single* leaf of any plant is the huge round lily pad of the Victoria water lily. One of these measured $8\frac{1}{2}$ feet (2.8 m) wide. A lily pad this size could easily support the weight of a 50-pound (22.5-kg) person.

Tallest Cactus

The tallest cactus in the world is the Saguaro cactus (*Cereus giganteus*). This giant plant lives in deserts in Arizona, southeastern California, and parts of Mexico. Its long, branching "arms" give it a unique appearance. One measured 52 feet (16 m) tall. An armless Saguaro found in Arizona was the tallest of all. Its tip was 78 feet (24 m) above the ground, higher than an eight-story apartment house.

SEE-ree-us jie-GANN-tee-us

A big gulper. Cacti have the ability to store what little water is available in their tissues. After it rains, the plant absorbs water and expands to a much larger size. Cacti have long, sharp spines that protect their juicy insides from hungry or thirsty desert creatures.

Home, safe home.
The Saguaro cactus is a snug homesite to small desert creatures. Woodpeckers and a tiny owl called the elf owl often dig nest holes high up on the cactus' arms and raise their families in spiny safety.

Biggest Fungus

Mushrooms and puffballs are plants known as fungi. They do not manufacture chlorophyll, so they are not green like most plants. Puffballs are among the largest of all fungi. The biggest puffball ever measured was a specimen of *Lycoperdon gigantea* found in England. This monster puffball was 64 inches (162 cm) around and 16 inches (40 cm) high, as big as an oil drum.

lie-CO-per-don jie-GAN-tee-yah

The biggest tree fungus ever found was a specimen of *Oxyporus nobilissimus* that measured 56 inches (140 cm) long by 37 inches (93 cm) wide. It weighed about 300 pounds (135 kg), about as much as a full-grown ostrich, the world's heaviest bird. Tree fungi are often called "bracket fungi" because they project from a tree's trunk like a bracket or shelf.

Largest Forest

The rainforests of the South American Amazon region cover an area about half the size of the continental United States, but they are not the world's largest forested area. That record belongs to the great forest of northern Russia and Siberia. These vast spruce and larch forests cover 2,700,000,000 acres (1,100 million hectares). They make up about 25 percent of the world's total forested area.

Largest Living Seaweed

The largest seaweed in the world is the giant kelp (*Macrocystis pyrifera*), which lives near rocky shores in the Pacific Ocean. The longest one ever measured was 196 feet (60 m) long. But some people have claimed to have seen giant kelp up to 1,000 feet (300 m) long.

Hangin' in there! Seaweeds are plants, but they are not "weeds" like those that live on land. They are *algae*.

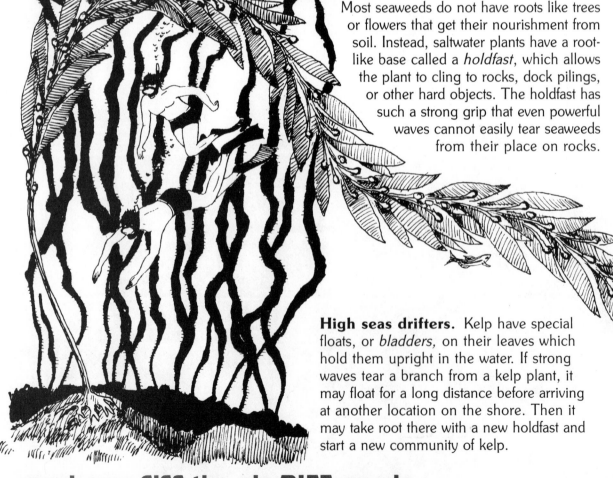

Most seaweeds do not have roots like trees or flowers that get their nourishment from soil. Instead, saltwater plants have a root-like base called a *holdfast*, which allows the plant to cling to rocks, dock pilings, or other hard objects. The holdfast has such a strong grip that even powerful waves cannot easily tear seaweeds from their place on rocks.

High seas drifters. Kelp have special floats, or *bladders,* on their leaves which hold them upright in the water. If strong waves tear a branch from a kelp plant, it may float for a long distance before arriving at another location on the shore. Then it may take root there with a new holdfast and start a new community of kelp.

mack-row-CISS-tiss pie-RIFF-err-ah

Underwater forest. The giant kelp grows in very thick forests near the shore. It can grow up to 18 inches (45 cm) in a single day. The tangled plants remind divers of underwater rain forests because the light is dim and thousands of fishes swirl about, looking like tropical birds flying through the trees.

Underwater jungle.
Sargassum weed drifts in great tangled masses, covering hundreds of square miles in the Atlantic Ocean. It is the largest mass of floating seaweed we know. The dense mat of drifting seaweed provides food and shelter to many small animals, including crabs, sea horses, baby fishes, and the strange sargassum fish.

Now you see it—now you don't! The sargassum fish's colors imitate the colors of the sargassum weed, and its body has tiny flaps and tabs of skin that look just like pieces of the weed.

Smallest Living Mammal

The smallest mammal is the pygmy white-toothed, or Etruscan, shrew (*Suncus etruscus*), which lives in Africa. It weighs 1.2 ounces (2.5 g), about as much as a quarter, and is only about 2 inches (4 cm) long, including its tiny tail. Think of how small its heart, lungs, and bones must be!

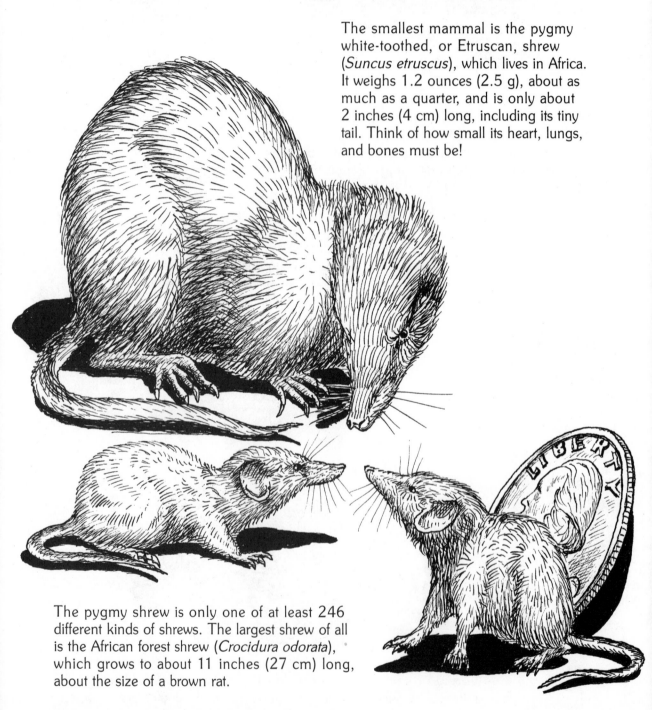

The pygmy shrew is only one of at least 246 different kinds of shrews. The largest shrew of all is the African forest shrew (*Crocidura odorata*), which grows to about 11 inches (27 cm) long, about the size of a brown rat.

SUN-kuss ee-TRUSS-kuss

Life on the fast track. Shrews really live life at high speed. They are constantly on the move, and their heart and lungs operate much faster than ours. Because of this, a shrew must eat constantly to supply its tiny body with energy. If it cannot find any food after about two hours, it may starve to death!

The shrew looks like a mouse, but it has very small eyes and sharp teeth. Shrews can kill and eat mice, even though a mouse is bigger. All shrews are members of a group of small mammals called *insectivores* because they eat worms, insects, and spiders.

Follow the leader.
Baby shrews follow their mother in a follow-the-leader line. Each baby grabs the back or tail of the one in front, and the first one in line holds on to the mother shrew.
Then they all march off through the grass in search of, what else? Food!

Smallest Living Mammal Babies

The mammal with the smallest babies looks like a mouse but isn't. The broad-footed marsupial mouse (*Neophascogale lorentzii*) of Australia gives birth to babies that are $16/100$ ths of an inch long and weigh about as much as a grain of sand!

Actual size of a new-born marsupial mouse

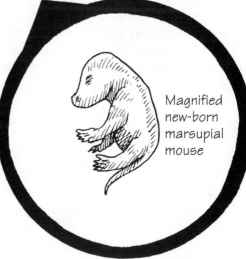

Magnified new-born marsupial mouse

When is a mouse not a mouse?

The marsupial mouse is a meat-eater, or carnivore, like a weasel or a cat. Mice, on the other hand, are rodents and have sharp, gnawing teeth designed to eat plants.

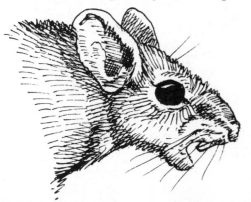

NEE-oh-fass-co-GAL-lay lorr-ENT-zee-eye

Marsupials are mammals whose babies are born only partly formed. The babies do not have eyes when they are born, and they must find their way to their mother's pouch by crawling through her belly fur. Once inside the pouch, they firmly attach themselves to a nipple and hang on to it. The babies live in the pouch until they have developed enough to survive on their own.

Most marsupials live in Australia. Kangaroos, wallabies, and koalas are familiar Australian marsupials. The common opossum (*Didelphis virginiana*) is a North American marsupial. When its babies leave their mother's pouch, they often hitch a ride on her back, sometimes hanging on to her tail with their own tiny tails.

Smallest Living Bird

Common bumblebee

The smallest of all birds is the Cuban bee hummingbird (*Mellisuga helenae*), which weighs less than a dime. Its tiny wings spread to a little more than the width of a quarter. This little bird, hardly bigger than a big bumblebee, uses its long bill to feed on nectar and insects in flowers.

Cuban bee hummingbird chasing a hawk

Cuban bee hummingbird

Corn flake

The bee hummingbird may be tiny, but it is not afraid of other birds, even hawks or owls. It chases much larger birds or even snakes away from its thimble-sized nest and pea-sized babies.

Not surprisingly, the bee hummingbird's egg is also the smallest bird egg known. It weighs about two-hundredths of an ounce. This is about as much as an average-sized corn flake.

mell-ih-SOO-gah HELL-enn-eye

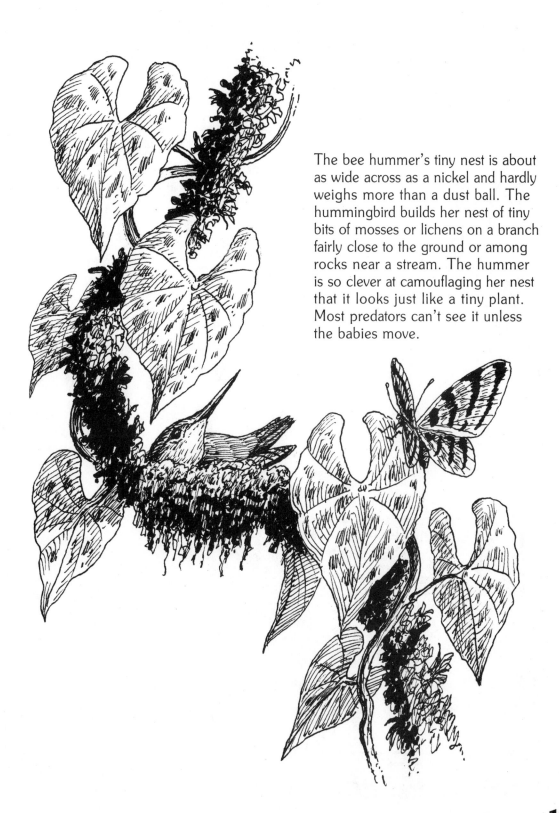

The bee hummer's tiny nest is about as wide across as a nickel and hardly weighs more than a dust ball. The hummingbird builds her nest of tiny bits of mosses or lichens on a branch fairly close to the ground or among rocks near a stream. The hummer is so clever at camouflaging her nest that it looks just like a tiny plant. Most predators can't see it unless the babies move.

Smallest Living Fish

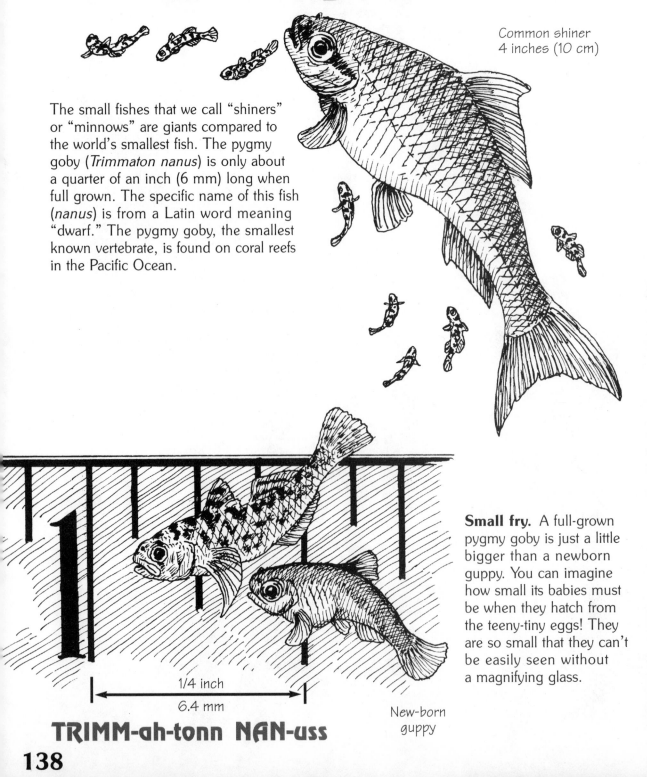

The small fishes that we call "shiners" or "minnows" are giants compared to the world's smallest fish. The pygmy goby (*Trimmaton nanus*) is only about a quarter of an inch (6 mm) long when full grown. The specific name of this fish (*nanus*) is from a Latin word meaning "dwarf." The pygmy goby, the smallest known vertebrate, is found on coral reefs in the Pacific Ocean.

Common shiner
4 inches (10 cm)

Small fry. A full-grown pygmy goby is just a little bigger than a newborn guppy. You can imagine how small its babies must be when they hatch from the teeny-tiny eggs! They are so small that they can't be easily seen without a magnifying glass.

1/4 inch
6.4 mm

TRIMM-ah-tonn NAN-uss

New-born guppy

138

Looking over your shoulder. Because it is so small, a pygmy goby is easy prey for other fishes that live on the coral reef. For this reason, most pygmy gobies stay very close to tiny holes and crevices in the reef. When they must move about, they look about cautiously and then zip from one hiding place to another with quick little jerks that are hard to follow with the eye.

Greatest Number of Eggs

Most species of fishes lay large numbers of eggs to make sure that as many young as possible survive. A large female codfish (*Gadus morhua*) may produce 1 million eggs during the breeding season, but that is not the world record for fish eggs. A big ocean sunfish (*Mola mola*) was estimated to have 300 million eggs! Each one measured .05-inch (1.3 mm), about the size of a pinhead.

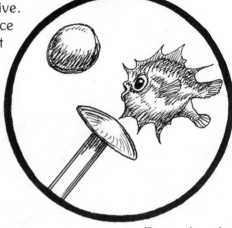

Egg and newly hatched young of the huge ocean sunfish

The world record for the fewest number of eggs is held by an African cichlid, *Haplochromis moori*. It lives in a large body of water called Lake Tanganyika, which is between Zaire and Tanzania in eastern Africa. The female may lay as few as 7 large eggs, which she hides and carefully guards in a small cave or grotto among the rocks of the lake bottom.

GADD-uss more-hoo-ah ● MOW-lah MOW-lah

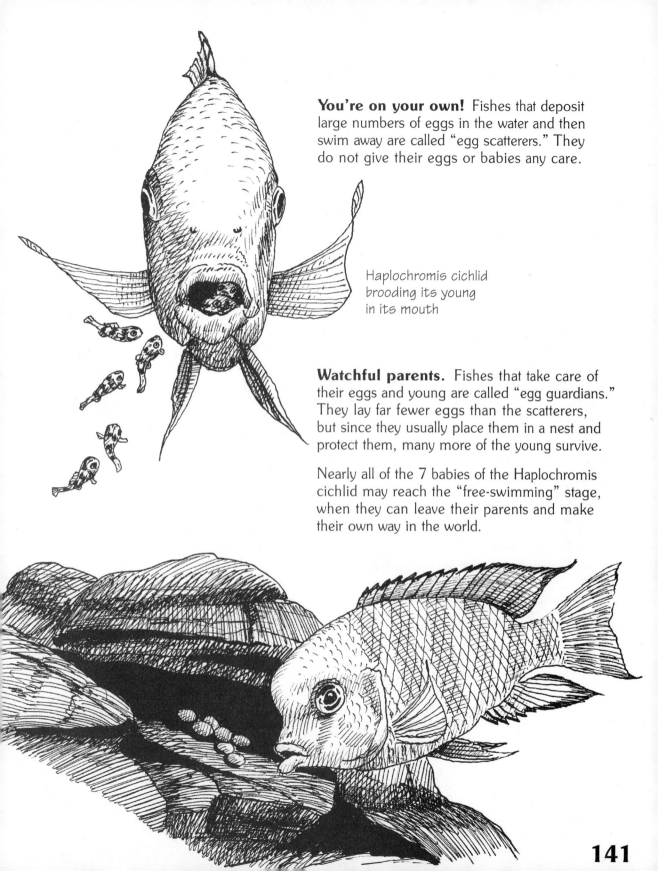

You're on your own! Fishes that deposit large numbers of eggs in the water and then swim away are called "egg scatterers." They do not give their eggs or babies any care.

Haplochromis cichlid
brooding its young
in its mouth

Watchful parents. Fishes that take care of their eggs and young are called "egg guardians." They lay far fewer eggs than the scatterers, but since they usually place them in a nest and protect them, many more of the young survive.

Nearly all of the 7 babies of the Haplochromis cichlid may reach the "free-swimming" stage, when they can leave their parents and make their own way in the world.

141

Smallest Living Snake

The huge anaconda, the world's largest snake, often reaches 25 feet (7.5 m) long, but it has a tiny relative that is only 5 inches (12 cm) long when full-grown and is as thin as a piece of string. That is why it is called the thread snake (*Leptotyphlops bilineata*). It lives on a few islands in the Caribbean Sea and eats very small animals, such as snails, insects, and worms.

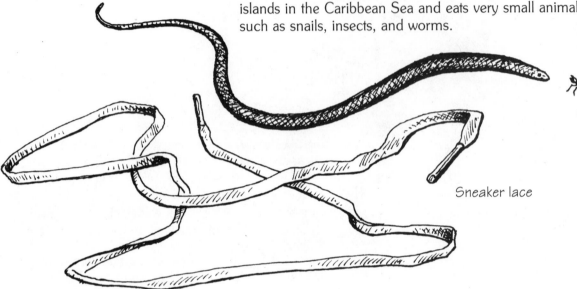

Ant

Sneaker lace

The ears have it. The thread snake burrows beneath the soil when it searches for its prey. Its eyes are very tiny and it is nearly blind, but it has an acute sense of hearing. It can sense, or "hear," the very soft vibrations of a worm moving in the earth nearby!

Head of thread snake

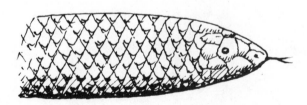

lepp-toe-TIE-flops bye-linn-ee-AH-TAH

North America's smallest snake, the little brown snake (*Storeria dekayi*), is about 15 inches (38 cm) long. That's three times as long as the thread snake, but it is still a half-pint. Brown snakes are very adaptable creatures and they are still common in suburbs and even cities, where they often live in weedy, vacant lots or under trash or pieces of wood or metal.

Open up! Most snakes can swallow prey much bigger than their mouths. A snake's jaw bones are very loosely connected, and the lower jaws unhinge and spread wide apart when the snake swallows a large animal. Since a snake does not have teeth for chewing, it must swallow its prey whole.

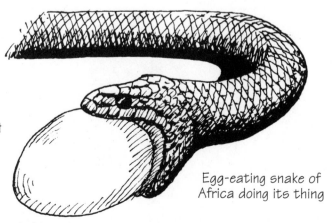

Egg-eating snake of Africa doing its thing

Smallest Living Reptile

The smallest reptile in the world is a tiny lizard called a gecko ('GEK-ho'). Many kinds of geckos live all over the world in warm tropical areas. The smallest is a wee creature called *Sphaerodactylus elasmorhynchus*. It lives in the Virgin Islands in the Caribbean Sea and is less than $1^1/_2$ inches (3 cm) long when it is full-grown. Its scientific name is much longer than it is!

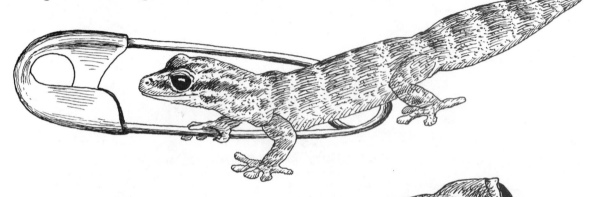

Geckos do not have eyelids like most lizards, so their eyes cannot be kept clean by blinking. Instead, the gecko uses its long tongue to wipe its eyes clean.

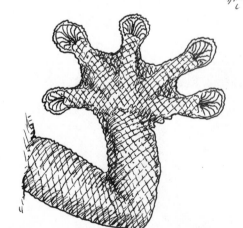

Fancy footwork. A gecko's foot is designed to help it scamper over walls, ceilings, and other smooth surfaces. The undersides of the toes have many bristles that end in tiny hooks. These hooks are so small that you need a microscope to see them. They catch on any rough spots on a wall or smooth tree trunk. Some geckos have toe bristles that end in tiny suction cups. These geckos can even run up a windowpane!

sfay-row-DAC-tee-luss ee-lass-more-HINK-uss

Geckos, like many other lizards, can break off their tails if they are grabbed by a predator. The tail grows back in a few weeks, but it is smaller than the original.

The incredible shrinking tail. The gecko uses its tail to store fat for energy when food is scarce. When there is plenty to eat, the gecko's tail is round and plump. If it cannot find enough to eat, it must withdraw its savings of fat and the tail shrinks down to a skinny strip.

Tokay, or house gecko
8 inches (20 cm)

smallest gecko

Hanging around the house. Most geckos live in forests where they hunt for insects at night. But some have learned that more bugs can be caught near lights in peoples' homes. In tropical areas these geckos are called *house geckos*. People often leave the screens off their windows because geckos are better bug killers than flyswatters.

Smallest Flowering Plant

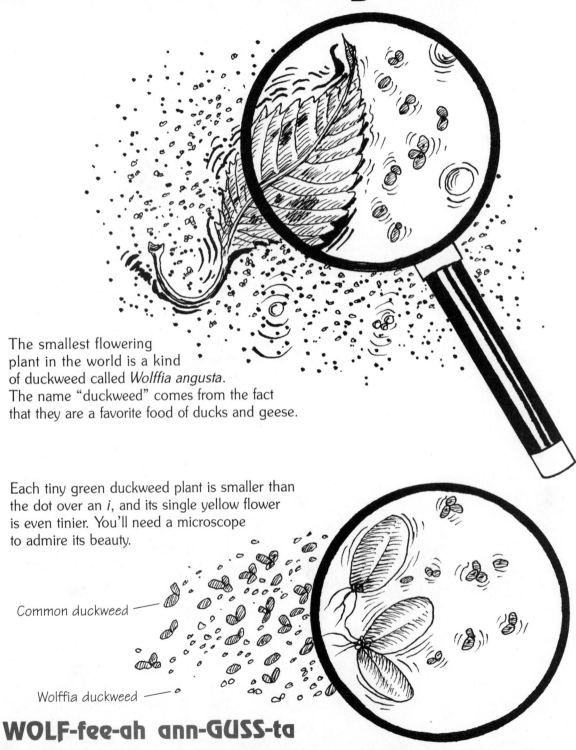

The smallest flowering
plant in the world is a kind
of duckweed called *Wolffia angusta*.
The name "duckweed" comes from the fact
that they are a favorite food of ducks and geese.

Each tiny green duckweed plant is smaller than
the dot over an *i*, and its single yellow flower
is even tinier. You'll need a microscope
to admire its beauty.

Common duckweed

Wolffia duckweed

WOLF-fee-ah ann-GUSS-ta

Fantastic floaters. Great numbers of duckweed float in thick carpets that may cover the entire water surface of a quiet pond or marsh. In fact, billions of duckweed plants may cover the water of a small pond. Sometimes the duckweed gets so thick that sunlight cannot reach other plants growing on the pond's bottom, but this happens only when there are not enough ducks or other plant-eating animals to eat the duckweed.

Save the wetlands. Although they can grow almost anywhere there are quiet waters, duckweed depends on freshwater wetlands for life. If wetlands are drained or filled with soil to make room for roads, houses, or shopping malls, the duckweed disappears and so do the ducks, geese, and other animals that use it for food.

Smallest Seed

Orchids have the world's smallest seeds. About 6 billion orchid seeds weigh an ounce. They easily float through the air from one place to another, where they take root and grow into new orchid plants.

One orchid, *Stelis graminea*, has flowers that are only .04 inch (1mm) wide. Other orchid flowers are shaped and colored like insects. The insects that look like the petals are attracted to these flowers and, by rubbing against them and spreading the plant's pollen, help fertilize the orchids.

STELL-iss gram-ih-NEE-yah

Orchids are referred to as *epiphytes*. This means that they depend on other plants, such as trees, for a place to grow. Most orchids live on the branches and trunks of trees in rain forests. If the trees are cut down or the forest is burned, the orchids are destroyed as well.

Some orchids grow on the ground. One orchid that lives on the forest floor in North America is the pink lady's slipper. Unfortunately, this plant's flower is so pretty that it is often picked or dug up by hikers or picnickers who find it in the woods. Because of this, it has become rare and is considered threatened in some places.

Smallest Living Things

Some of the very smallest things in the world are bacteria and tiny animals called *protozoa*. Protozoa means "first animals." Bacteria and protozoa are so small that they cannot be seen without a microscope.

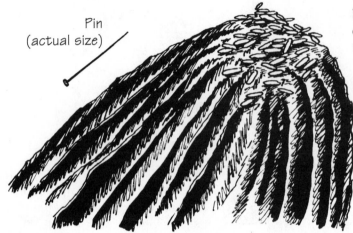

Pin
(actual size)

Rod-shaped bacteria on the head of a pin magnified 100 times

Good guys, bad guys. Many thousands of bacteria could fit on a pinhead. Some kinds of bacteria can cause serious diseases, while others help us make medicines, such as antibiotics, and foods, such as cheese.

A variety of bacteria magnified 100 times

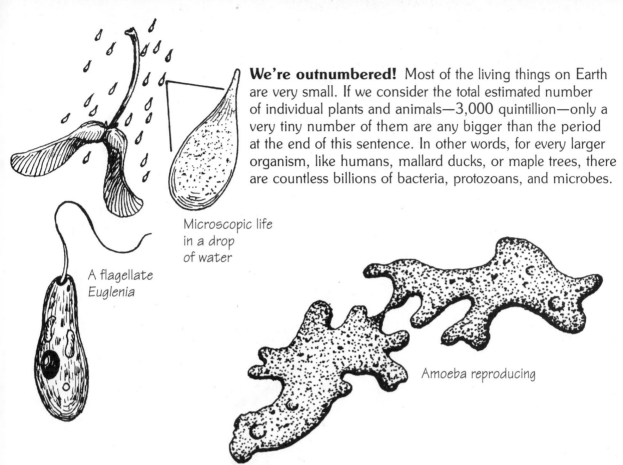

We're outnumbered! Most of the living things on Earth are very small. If we consider the total estimated number of individual plants and animals—3,000 quintillion—only a very tiny number of them are any bigger than the period at the end of this sentence. In other words, for every larger organism, like humans, mallard ducks, or maple trees, there are countless billions of bacteria, protozoans, and microbes.

Microscopic life in a drop of water

A flagellate Euglenia

Amoeba reproducing

Plant or animal? Protozoa are one-celled animals. Protozoans live in the sea, or in ponds, lakes, and rivers. One kind, the amoeba, moves about by changing its shape. It reproduces by simply dividing into two separate animals.

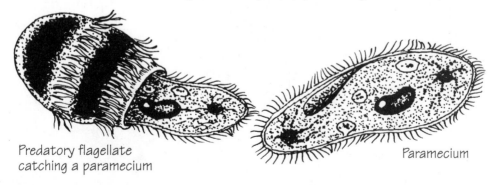

Predatory flagellate catching a paramecium

Paramecium

Some protozoans, such as the paramecium, wave tiny hairs, called cilia, like little oars to get around. This tiny creature looks something like the sole of a shoe, so it is sometimes called the *slipper animalcule*. Another microscopic animal, the *flagellate*, uses a whip-like thread to propel itself along. There may be hundreds of these microscopic critters paddling around in a single drop of pond water.

Smallest Living Crustacean

The smallest of all crustaceans is *Alonella*, a kind of water flea. A big adult can be 0.0098 of an inch (0.25 mm) long. Water fleas live in fresh water and are common in small ponds or swamps. They are not insects and are called "fleas" only because they are so small and look something like the biting fleas that annoy dogs, cats, and people.

Dog flea

Alonella

Actual size

AL-on-ELL-ah

Big biter. The largest true flea is *Hystrichopsylla schefferi*, which bites wild mammals but not humans. The females are larger than the males. One female flea found in the nest of a rodent measured ¼-inch (8 mm) wide. That's about the diameter of an ordinary pencil.

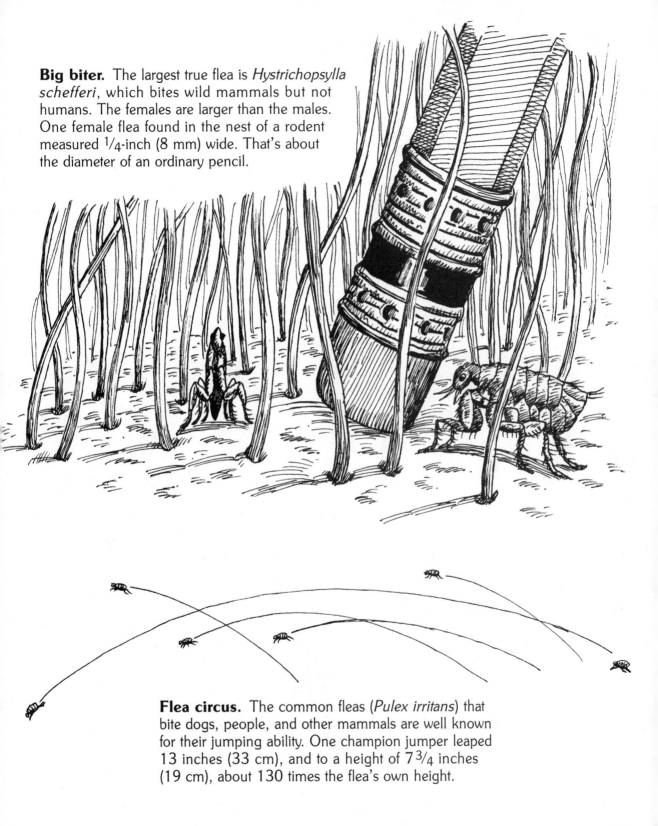

Flea circus. The common fleas (*Pulex irritans*) that bite dogs, people, and other mammals are well known for their jumping ability. One champion jumper leaped 13 inches (33 cm), and to a height of 7¾ inches (19 cm), about 130 times the flea's own height.

Fastest Living Creature

The spine-tailed swift (*Hirundapus caudacutus*) of Asia is the fastest flying bird *and* the fastest of all living creatures. It is about the size of a sparrow and flies at 106 miles per hour (170 kph). Obviously, swifts have no trouble catching the fastest insects.

Another speedy swift, the chimney swift of North America, can fly at about 60 miles per hour (96 kph). This bird formerly lived in hollow trees but soon discovered that house chimneys make even better homes. They live in the chimneys only during the summer when buildings are not being heated.

hi-roon-DAPP-uss caw-dah-KEW-tuss

The peregrine falcon is another fast flyer. This speedy hawk can cruise along at 100 miles per hour (160 kph) and dive at more than 200 miles per hour (320 kph). This beautiful falcon is now considered an endangered species.

Among the insects, the deer bot fly, found near farms and fields, is the fastest flyer. The fly can easily cruise at 24 miles per hour (39 kph), but it can "power up" to 36 miles per hour (58 kph). Horses and cattle are so afraid of the painful bite of bot flies that they race wildly away as soon as one comes near.

Fastest Living Mammal

The fastest mammal in the world is a cat—the cheetah, or hunting leopard (*Acinonyx jubatus*). Its long legs carry it at top speeds of nearly 65 miles per hour (100 kph).

All pooped out. Like most cats, the cheetah is not a long-distance runner. The cat sneaks up on its prey and tries to get as close as it can before attempting to catch it. The cheetah can run faster than the small antelopes it eats, but if it doesn't catch them within a distance of about four city blocks, it gives up the chase.

ay-sinn-ON-ix joo-BAT-uss

Born to run. The pronghorn antelope (*Antilocapra americana*) is the fastest mammal in North America. While it is not a world record holder for speed, the pronghorn can run fast for a much longer distance than the cheetah, sprinting for more than 4 miles (7 km) at an average speed of 35 miles per hour (50 kph).

Pretty doggone fast! Some long-legged dogs are also fast runners. The greyhound (*Canis familiaris*) is not as fast as the cheetah, but it can run for much longer distances at over 40 miles per hour (60 kph). Long ago, these dogs were used to hunt other swift animals like deer and gazelles.

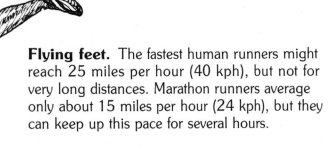

Flying feet. The fastest human runners might reach 25 miles per hour (40 kph), but not for very long distances. Marathon runners average only about 15 miles per hour (24 kph), but they can keep up this pace for several hours.

Fastest Living Fish

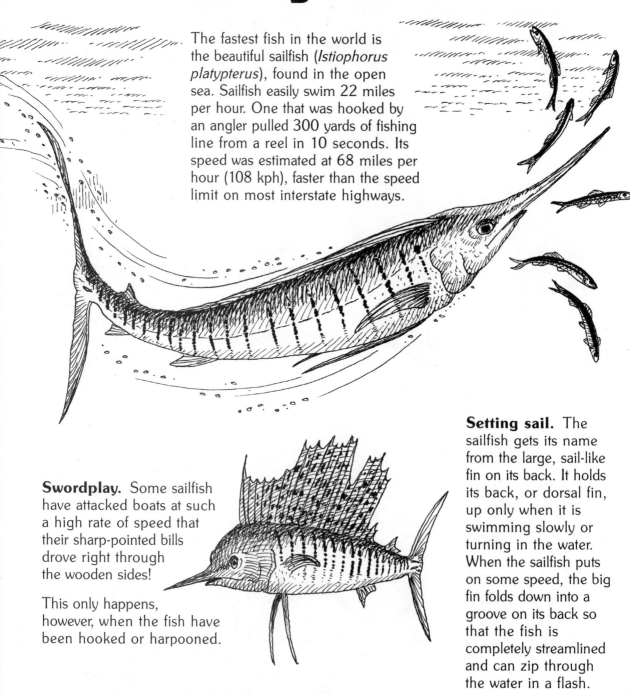

The fastest fish in the world is the beautiful sailfish (*Istiophorus platypterus*), found in the open sea. Sailfish easily swim 22 miles per hour. One that was hooked by an angler pulled 300 yards of fishing line from a reel in 10 seconds. Its speed was estimated at 68 miles per hour (108 kph), faster than the speed limit on most interstate highways.

Swordplay. Some sailfish have attacked boats at such a high rate of speed that their sharp-pointed bills drove right through the wooden sides!

This only happens, however, when the fish have been hooked or harpooned.

Setting sail. The sailfish gets its name from the large, sail-like fin on its back. It holds its back, or dorsal fin, up only when it is swimming slowly or turning in the water. When the sailfish puts on some speed, the big fin folds down into a groove on its back so that the fish is completely streamlined and can zip through the water in a flash.

iss-tee-OFF-orr-uss pla-TIPP-terr-uss

Fishy aviators. Flying fishes (*Cypselurus heterurus*) are also pretty speedy animals. Their long, stiff pectoral fins act like wings when the fish leaps out of the water and skims over the waves. Flying fishes have been clocked at 45 miles per hour (72 kph) when speeding up for a takeoff.

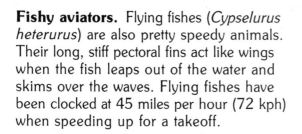

The PT Bird. Not all speedy swimmers are fishes. Penguins cannot fly in the air, but they use their wings to "fly" underwater at a pretty good clip. The fastest swimmer among penguins is the gentoo penguin (*Pygocelis papua*). One was clocked at 17 miles per hour (27 kph), a little faster than the average speed of a cruise ship.

Fastest Living Reptile

Lizards are the fastest reptiles in the world, and the fastest of them all is the spiny-tailed iguana (*Ctenosaura similis*) of Costa Rica. It has been clocked at almost 22 miles per hour (35 kph). That may be a slow speed in a moving car, but it's pretty fast for a lizard running through a thick jungle.

Scaly streakers. The fastest lizards in North America are racerunners found in the southeastern United States. Some can run up to 20 miles per hour (32 kph).

TEE-no-saw-rah SIMM-ill-uss

Marathon racerunner. There are several kinds of racerunners, but the fastest is the six-lined racerunner (*Cnemidophorus sexlineatus*), which lives in North Carolina and Georgia. This speed champ has been clocked at 21 miles per hour (34 kph). It even has six colorful "racing stripes" on its back and sides!

Slowest Living Animal

Some animals move so slowly that they hold world records, too. The common pond snail, *Physa*, moves along at only about 23 inches (56 cm) per hour. The little gray carnivorous slug is a little faster. It crawls at about 3 feet (1 m) per hour. At that speed, it would take the slug 73 days to go one mile.

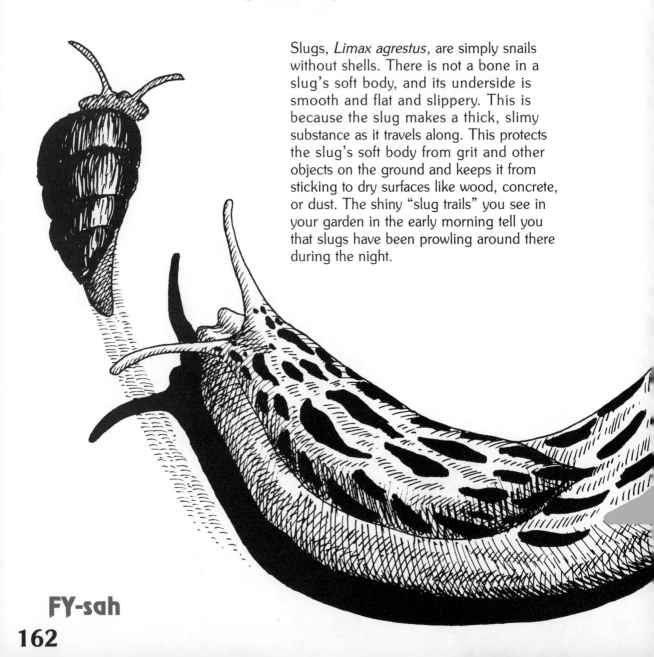

Slugs, *Limax agrestus*, are simply snails without shells. There is not a bone in a slug's soft body, and its underside is smooth and flat and slippery. This is because the slug makes a thick, slimy substance as it travels along. This protects the slug's soft body from grit and other objects on the ground and keeps it from sticking to dry surfaces like wood, concrete, or dust. The shiny "slug trails" you see in your garden in the early morning tell you that slugs have been prowling around there during the night.

FY-sah

Beautiful creeper. Most slugs are not very colorful or what we would consider attractive, but there is one exception. The golden slug lives in the damp forests of Washington, Oregon, and California. It is about 6 inches (15 cm) long and is a bright reddish-gold color. It looks like a little candle flame when it crawls over the dark green moss of the forest floor.

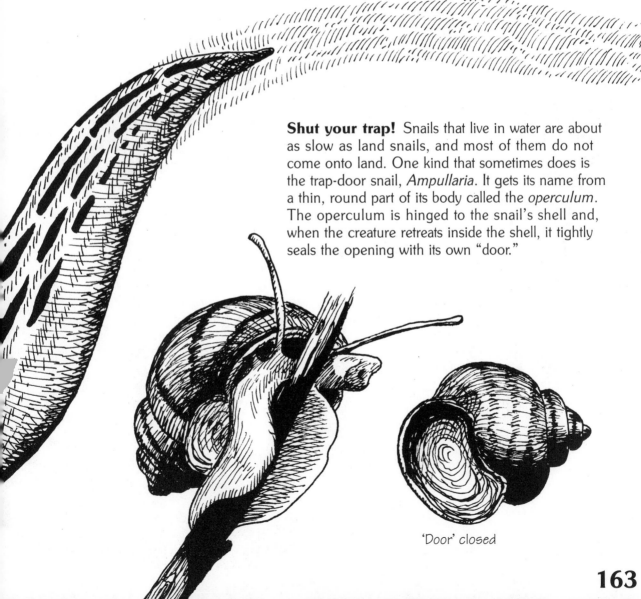

Shut your trap! Snails that live in water are about as slow as land snails, and most of them do not come onto land. One kind that sometimes does is the trap-door snail, *Ampullaria*. It gets its name from a thin, round part of its body called the *operculum*. The operculum is hinged to the snail's shell and, when the creature retreats inside the shell, it tightly seals the opening with its own "door."

'Door' closed

Slowest Living Mammal

The slowest mammal in the world is the three-toed sloth (*Bradypus tridactylus*) of South America. These sleepy creatures live in trees and move around at about 6 feet (1.8 m) per minute. It would take a sloth about 42 days to travel a mile. Simple green plants called algae often grow on the sloth's fur, so that the animal looks like a bunch of moss hanging in the tree.

Vanishing rain forests. Sloths and many other rain forest animals are becoming less common as their forest homes are cut down for lumber or burned to make room for farms. Sloths spend their entire lives in trees and are so slow-moving that when the trees are cut down, they cannot flee to other parts of the forest. They are often killed for food or captured for pets.

BRAY-dee-puss try-DAC-tee-luss

ZZZZZZ.
The three-toed sloth is also one of the champion
sleepers of the world. Sloths still spend about 80
percent of their lives sleeping up in the trees!

Slowest to Bloom

Late bloomer. Most plants bloom every year, but not the slowest bloomer on the planet. The puya, or century plant (*Puya raimondii*), takes about 150 years to bloom! When it does, it sends up a tall stalk, called a *panicle*.

POO-yah ray-MON-dee-eye

The panicle is 35 feet (10.7 m) high, as tall as a utility pole, and bears about 8,000 small white flowers at its tip. Soon after it blooms, the plant dies. The puya lives high in the mountains of Bolivia in South America.

Herb heavyweight. The puya is the world's largest herb. Herbs like sage, thyme, and pepper have been used as food and flavoring for thousands of years.

Keeping a low profile. Many trees take 50 or 60 years to reach their full size. But one Sitka spruce tree, *Picea sitchensis*, took 98 years to reach 11 inches (28 cm) tall! This tree lived on the tundra in Canada, a flat, very cold environment near the Arctic Circle.

167

Fastest Wingbeat

Wings of steel. Midges, *Chironomids*, beat their wings more than a thousand times per second—62,000 times per minute!

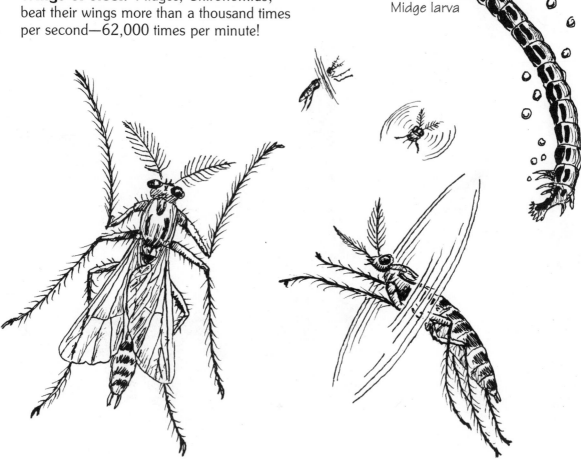

Midge larva

A feathered buzz-bomb. Some world records come from the way an animal gets around. A hummingbird's wings twist in its shoulder sockets and rotate like helicopter blades. This allows the bird to hover motionless in one place and even fly backwards, something no other bird can do.

keer-oh-NO-mids

Swallowtail
caterpillar

Loafin' along. The record holder for the *slowest*
wingbeat among the insects is the swallowtail butterfly
(*Papilio*). Although it can flap along pretty quickly
when it is frightened, the average wingbeat of these
large butterflies is a mere 300 beats per minute.

Highest Altitude of Any Bird

Sometimes, where an animal lives or has been observed by people sets a world record. Most of the earth's plants and animals live close to the level of the oceans because the climate is milder and there is more food and water. But some creatures have been seen high up in mountains where the air is thin and very cold and most of the water is frozen.

A vulture hit an airplane at 37,000 feet—more than 8 miles (14 km) up in the sky. Another pilot spotted a flock of swans flying by at 27,000 feet (8,230 m).

BOO-fo terr-ESS-triss

A common toad (*Bufo terrestris*) was found living on a mountainside at 26,000 feet (7,900 m). Toads can often survive cold and dry conditions if they burrow down into the soil.

The yak, *Bos grunniens*, a kind of Asian wild cattle, often climbs 20,000 feet (6,100 m) in mountains when it's browsing for food.

Biggest Living Millipede

The millipede, whose name means "thousand-footed," has more legs than any other animal. But no millipede has anywhere near a thousand legs. Actually, it may have as few as eight and up to 700. The average number is 100 legs. Most millipedes have four legs per each segment of its body.

You can find these harmless creatures in your garden or among fallen leaves in the woods.

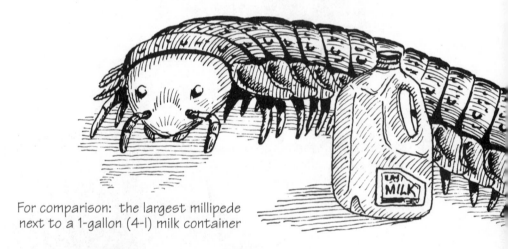

For comparison: the largest millipede next to a 1-gallon (4-l) milk container

arr-throw-PLOO-rah

Creepy crawler. Most millipedes are small animals about an inch or two long. But *Arthropleura*, an extinct kind that lived about 220 million years ago in the Carboniferous Period, had about 45 pairs of legs and was nearly 6 feet (1.8 m) long! This huge millipede was the largest invertebrate (animal without a backbone) ever to walk on land.

Mild-mannered. Millipedes are harmless creatures that live on plants and other matter they find on the forest floor. They move slowly and do not have mouths that can bite or sting, so the only way they can protect themselves from predators is to coil tightly into a spiral with their head in the center. But their best defense is to remain out of sight under leaves and logs.

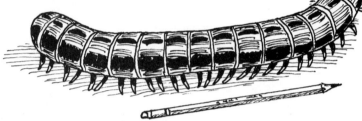

For comparison: an ordinary 8-inch (20-cm) lead pencil

Out of Africa. The largest millipede alive today is the giant African millipede, *Graphidostreptus gigas*. It may reach 14 inches (35 cm) long. This big but harmless millipede is popular as a pet.

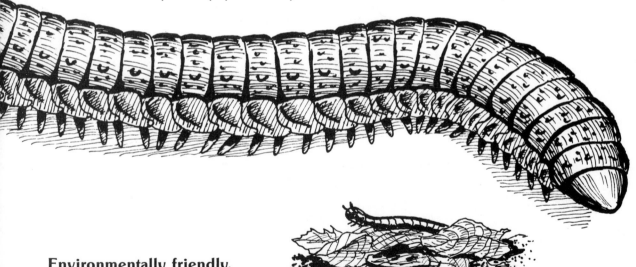

Environmentally friendly. Scientists think that millipedes are among nature's best recyclers. They eat decomposing plants and recycle their nutrients back into the soil. Special chemicals called *enzymes* help them digest wood, which few other animals can eat.

Longest Jump

The red kangaroo (*Macropus rufus*) of Australia holds the long-jump world record. It can jump more than 40 feet (12 m)! That's longer than four compact cars parked end-to-end. The 'roo can't make such a long jump from a standstill, though. It has to get a long, hopping headstart.

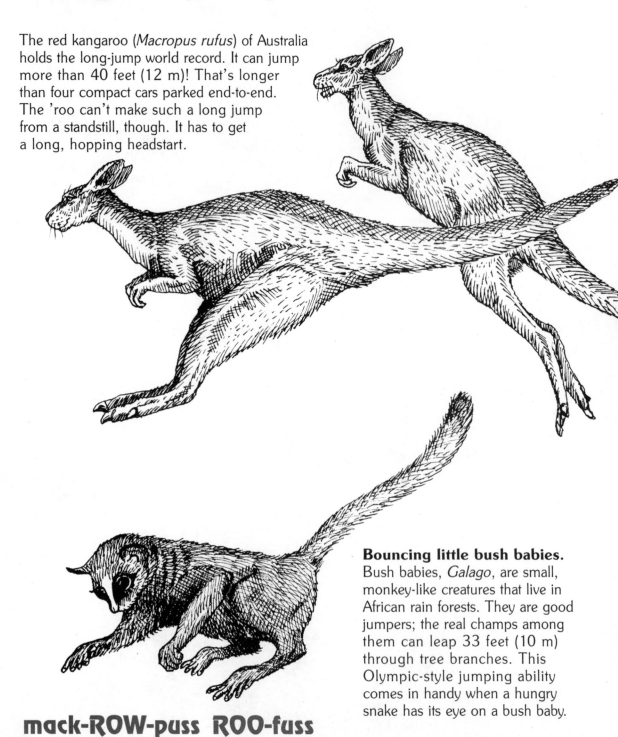

mack-ROW-puss ROO-fuss

Bouncing little bush babies. Bush babies, *Galago*, are small, monkey-like creatures that live in African rain forests. They are good jumpers; the real champs among them can leap 33 feet (10 m) through tree branches. This Olympic-style jumping ability comes in handy when a hungry snake has its eye on a bush baby.

Superfrog! But the jumping record compared to size is held by a little frog from Africa called the sharp-nosed frog, *Rana oxyrhyncha*. It is only about 3 inches (10 cm) long, but it can jump more than 15 feet (4.6 m) in one jump—a long, long distance for such a tiny creature. A 5-foot (1.5-m)-tall person would have to jump about 360 feet (119 m)—from a standstill—to equal this record! One of these little frogs jumped more than 33 feet (10 m) in three one-after-the-other jumps.

Pouncing puma. The documented high-jump record is held by a mammal—the puma, or mountain lion, *Felis concolor*. One of these big cats jumped 23 feet (7 m) straight up from a standstill. To equal this jump, you would have to stand in one spot and then leap about 30 feet (9 m)—to the peak of the roof on an average house. The puma often leaps up into trees if it is chased.

Longest-distance Flier

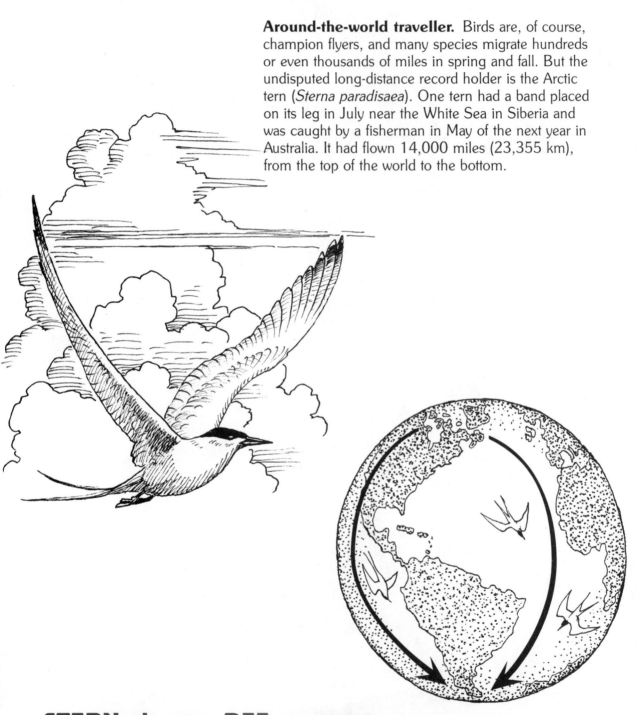

Around-the-world traveller. Birds are, of course, champion flyers, and many species migrate hundreds or even thousands of miles in spring and fall. But the undisputed long-distance record holder is the Arctic tern (*Sterna paradisaea*). One tern had a band placed on its leg in July near the White Sea in Siberia and was caught by a fisherman in May of the next year in Australia. It had flown 14,000 miles (23,355 km), from the top of the world to the bottom.

STERN-ah para-DEE-see-eye

Fly away home. The world record for nonstop flying is held by the sooty tern (*Sterna fuscata*) of the tropical Atlantic Ocean. This tern flies continuously for *3 to 4 years* after leaving its nest as an adult, before returning to its island homes to breed. Terns sometimes land briefly on the surface of the sea as they feed, so the sooty tern may do this when nobody's looking.

Oldest Living Thing

The oldest known living organism is a tree, the bristlecone pine (*Pinus aristata*). One bristlecone near the Pacific Ocean in California is believed to be about 4,900 years old. It was young when the ancient Egyptians were building the pyramids. The bristlecone pine often lives where it is exposed to strong winds and salt from the ocean, which makes it grow twisted and gnarled as it gets older.

PIE-nuss arr-ih-STAT-ah

Tough old bird. An Andean condor, *Vultur gryphus*, a kind of vulture, lived for more than 72 years in a large zoo cage in the Moscow Zoo in Russia. The vulture was brought to the zoo as an adult in 1892 and died in 1964.

Oldtimer tortoises. The animals that live the longest are the huge, 700-pound (300-kg) tortoises (*Geochelone gigantea*) that live on the Galapagos Islands in the Pacific Ocean and on the island of Aldabra in the Indian Ocean. These tortoises have been known to live 150 years in captivity.

Most Abundant Wild Bird

Some animals set world records because there are so many of them. There are probably many, many billions or even trillions of small animals like insects, though we cannot count them all. But birds can be counted—or at least estimated more easily. Scientists have calculated that a small African finch, the red-billed quelea (*Quelea quelea*), is the most abundant wild bird in the world. There are at least 1½ billion of them, about one-sixth the number of all the people on earth.

Ganging up. Like many birds that flock together in great numbers, queleas can cause a lot of damage to food crops in Africa. Because of this, farmers kill about 200 million of them each year, but it hardly makes a dent in their numbers!

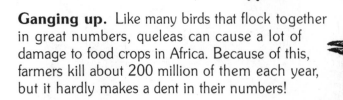

kwee-LEE-ah kwee-LEE-ah

Feathered noisemakers. The red-winged blackbird (*Aegalius phoenicopterus*) is probably the most abundant wild bird in North America. There are between 30 and 50 million of these familiar birds. Red-wings gather in huge flocks in the fall, mostly near marshes. When they come together in roosts with starlings and other blackbirds, the noise is so loud it can be heard at least a mile away.

Super-flock. The domestic chicken (*Gallus gallus*) is the most abundant bird of all. At any time, there are more than 8 billion chickens alive on farms or chicken ranches all over the world.

We're not alone! Some scientists have estimated that we humans share the Earth with 3,000,000,000,000,000,000,000,000,000,000,000,000—that's 3,000 quintillion—other living organisms. Most of these are organisms like bacteria, microbes, insects, and the 10,000 known species of worms.

Most Abundant Insect

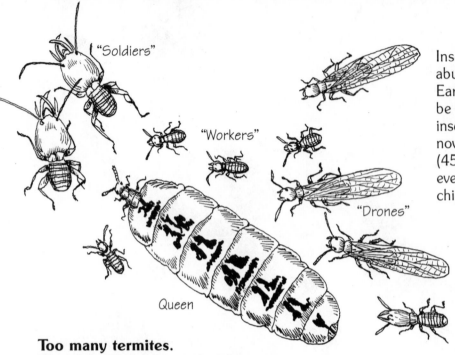

"Soldiers"

"Workers"

"Drones"

Queen

Insects are the most abundant animals on Earth. And termites may be the most abundant insects of all. There are now about one-half ton (453 kg) of termites for every man, woman, and child on Earth!

Too many termites.

There have always been a lot of termites of many different kinds all over the planet, but now there are even more—a lot more. This is because people have cut down hundreds of thousands of acres of forests, so there is now more dead wood lying around for termites to eat. Scientists say there has been a termite "population explosion" over the past 20 years.

Wood butchers. Most termites have special bacteria, called "anaerobic" bacteria, in their intestines that allow them to digest wood fibers. "Anaerobic" means that the bacteria are able to live without oxygen.

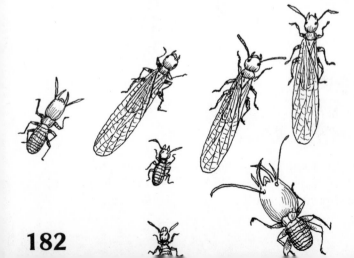

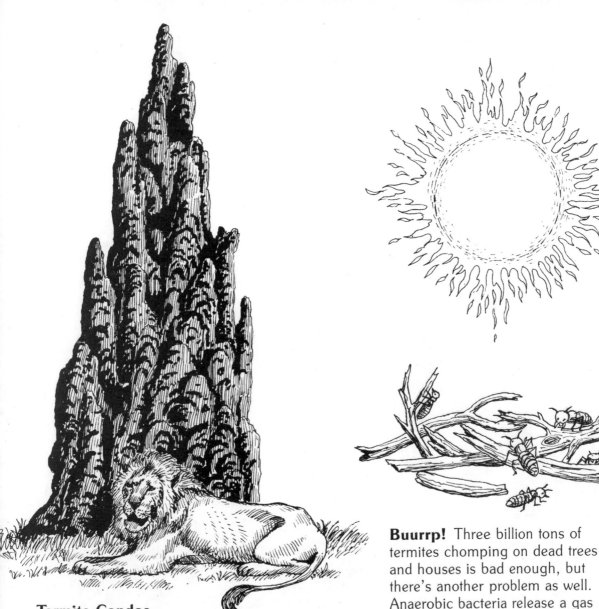

Termite Condos.

African termites are among the best house builders in the world. Their mounds are made of termite saliva mixed with wood particles and soil. When this mixture dries, it is as hard as concrete. The mounds have hundreds of narrow passageways and are actually a great "city" of termites. A big termite mound can be more than 20 feet (6 m) high, and up to 10 million termites may live there. If African termites were as big as people, a mound that high would be four times taller than New York City's Empire State Building!

Buurrp! Three billion tons of termites chomping on dead trees and houses is bad enough, but there's another problem as well. Anaerobic bacteria release a gas called methane when they help the termites digest the wood. This gas rises up into the upper atmosphere, where it traps radiation from the sun. This prevents some of the sun's heat from escaping from the Earth.

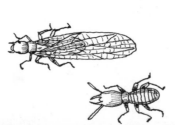

183

Biggest Natural Pothole

The pothole that ate Pennsylvania. Potholes in streets and highways are created when water and ice damage a roadway, then cars and trucks repeatedly hit the damaged spots. The biggest *natural* pothole in the world is a big hole in the side of a hill. It was discovered at Archbold, Pennsylvania, in 1881. Coal miners using dynamite uncovered the big hole in the ground, which measured 42 feet (13 m) wide and 50 feet (15 m) deep. The pothole had been formed by the heavy ice of a glacier thousands of years ago.

A bottomless pit. This giant pothole was filled with hundreds of tons of smooth, rounded pebbles that the ice had carried with it and that had scoured out the circular pothole. The miners carted away 300 wagonloads of pebbles before the pothole was finally empty!

el kan-YON day KOL-ka

Carving out a canyon. The largest gorge, or canyon, on Earth is the Grand Canyon in the North American West. This magnificent canyon follows the course of the Colorado River for 217 miles (349 km) in the state of Arizona. It varies from 4 to 13 miles (6–20 km) in width and is 5,300 feet (1,615 m) deep.

For millions of years the Colorado River flowed through the rocks, carrying tons of silt, sand, and rocks. The friction of the water and material it carried gradually wore a gully through the hard rock. Little by little, the river's bed sank lower and lower until the result was the spectacular gorge.

Almost bottomless pit?
The deepest pit in the world is
El Cañon de Colca in Peru, South America.
This great gorge is 10,607 feet (3,223 m) deep at its lowest part.

185

Biggest Desert

The world's biggest sandbox. The desert with the most dunes and sand in the world is the 350,000-square-mile (906,500-sq.-km) Takia Makan Desert in China. This desert's Mongolian name— "takia makan"—means "once you go in, you never come out."

Tack-EYE-yah Mack-AN

Life's a beach. The highest sand dunes in the world are found in the Algerian desert in North Africa. One dune measured more than 1,400 feet (430 m) high. That's as tall as the twin towers of the World Trade Center in New York City.

One endless beach. The largest sandy island in the world is Frazer Island near Queensland, Australia. This island is not much more than a single giant sand dune 75 miles (120 km) long.

Dunes look a lot like big mountains made of sand but, unlike ordinary mountains, they can move. Sand dunes in the Sahara Desert of Africa have been clocked at up to 50 feet (15 m) per year. That probably doesn't seem like much of a speed record until you consider the millions of tons of sand the wind has to push along to make the dune move.

Biggest Known Natural Explosion

Megabang. Bombs made by people can explode with tremendous force, but nature can create even bigger blasts. One of the most powerful explosions in history took place in 1815 on an island in the Java Sea. There, a 13,000-foot (3,900-m) -high mountain called Tambora suddenly blew its volcanic top. The blast was heard on other islands nearly 800 miles (1,288 km) away.

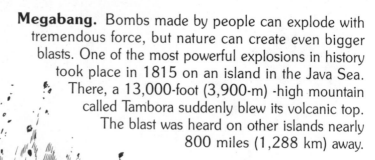

Chill out! The Tambora explosion spewed about 170 billion tons of dust into the atmosphere. This dust hid the sun for 300 miles (483 km) around the volcano and finally spread all over the Earth. It created beautiful sunsets everywhere, but it also caused cooler temperatures in Europe and North America. The year 1815 was so cold that it was called "the year without summer."

Crack-ah-TAU

A sleeping giant. Another volcano, Krakatau, set a record for the loudest bang ever recorded. Krakatau is on a small Indonesian island in the Indian Ocean. When it erupted in 1883, the noise was heard 3,000 miles (4,830 km) away. Scientists using special instruments recorded the explosion's shock wave circling the Earth six times. Like many volcanos, Krakatau had been quiet for so long that people living nearby never gave a thought to any danger. For them, it had just been a big mountain for more than 200 years.

Fastest Glacier

When we think of glaciers, we usually think of huge masses of ice moving so slowly that their movement can't be measured. But the Steele Glacier in the Yukon in Canada has set the record for the fastest moving glacier. In the summer of 1966, it moved at the speed of 2 feet (60 cm) per hour. When it stopped moving a year later, it had traveled more than 6 miles (10 km).

Giant snowdrifts. Glaciers begin as snow that becomes packed down and heavier as years pass. To qualify as a true glacier, an ice "sheet" must be at least 60 feet (18 m) thick. When the ice becomes this thick, it is very heavy and may begin to move.

Getting moving. What makes a glacier move? Once the ice is heavy enough, it slides over the ground if the land slopes downward and there is water between the ice and the ground. The water acts like grease, helping the ice slide more easily over rock and soil. When glaciers move, they often look like rivers of ice.

BEAR-ing GLAY-shur

At the end of the last Ice Age, about 12,000 years ago, more than 20 percent of the Earth's land was covered by ice. Today, only 9.7 percent of the Earth is covered by thick, permanent ice. The continent of Antarctica has the most (86 percent), and Greenland has the rest (11 percent).

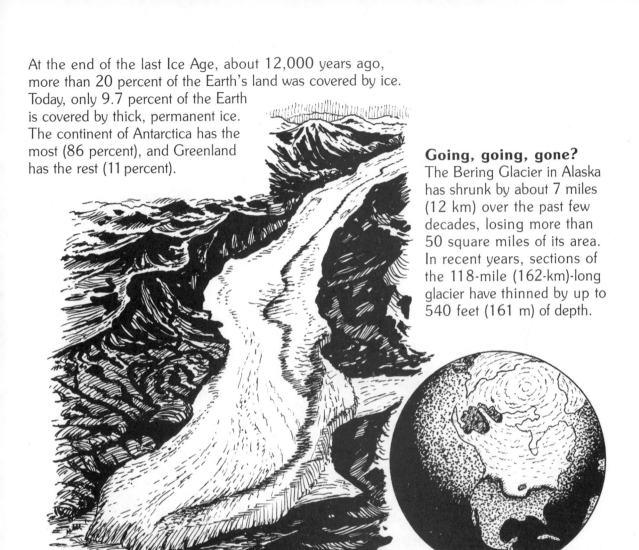

Going, going, gone?
The Bering Glacier in Alaska has shrunk by about 7 miles (12 km) over the past few decades, losing more than 50 square miles of its area. In recent years, sections of the 118-mile (162-km)-long glacier have thinned by up to 540 feet (161 m) of depth.

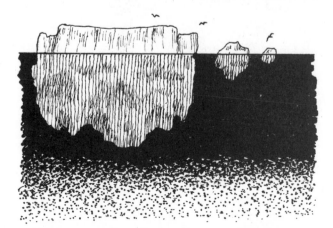

Baby bergs. Where the edge of a glacier is near the sea, large pieces sometimes break off and float away. When this happens, the glacier is said to be *calving*. These big ice chunks are called *bergs*. The ocean near a glacier may be filled with large and small icebergs. Only about 10 percent of a floating iceberg is above the surface of the water.

Biggest Wave

Storms at sea can produce big waves. The biggest wave ever was 112 feet (33.7 m) high, measured from the pilot house of a ship sailing through a powerful hurricane in the Pacific Ocean. Observers noted that the wave was higher than the tallest mast on the ship.

Waves created by volcanoes erupting underwater are usually not as high as surface waves, but they can often be much more dangerous. They are called *seismic waves*, or tsunamis. Very strong tsunamis can cross the ocean at speeds of 500 miles per hour, faster than a jet plane. One tsunami that struck Japan in 1896 destroyed 170 miles (280 km) of coastline and killed 28,000 people. This wave was 75 feet (23 m) high.

su-NAM-ees

Fast-forward tides. The tide usually goes out and comes back in—or ebbs and flows—slowly. But in some places it can move fast. Then it is called a *tidal bore*. Tidal bores up to six feet deep have been clocked at 15 miles per hour (25 kph) on the Amazon River in South America. That's about as fast as the average person can run. The famous tidal bore at Mont Saint Michel in France can move as fast as a horse can gallop—about 28 mph (58 kph). The edge of this tidal bore may be just a few inches deep, or it may rush across the wide sand flats like a great, wide wave.

Longest River

The longest river in the world is the Nile River of Africa. The Nile begins near Lake Victoria in East Africa and flows 4,160 miles (6,680 km) north to Egypt, where it enters the Red Sea. In 1977, a huge dam was built across the river at Aswan in Egypt, to generate electricity and to irrigate dry land.

Looking for the faucet. For a long time no one knew where the Nile River's beginning, or source, was. Finally, an explorer found the river's source 250 miles (400 km) up a much smaller river called the Kagera. He discovered that the world's greatest river began in a few tiny springs that trickled down a hillside into a rocky ravine.

Kah-GAIR-ah

The Big A. The Amazon River
is the world's second longest river.
It is 4,000 miles (6,437 km) long.
The Amazon begins in Peru and
crosses nearly all of South America
from west to east before emptying
into the Atlantic Ocean in Brazil.

Trickle, trickle. The world's shortest
true, free-flowing river is the D River in
Lincoln City, Oregon. It connects a
small seaside lake to the Pacific Ocean
and is only 440 feet (134 m) long.

Biggest Asteroid

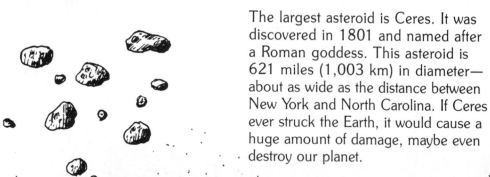

The largest asteroid is Ceres. It was discovered in 1801 and named after a Roman goddess. This asteroid is 621 miles (1,003 km) in diameter—about as wide as the distance between New York and North Carolina. If Ceres ever struck the Earth, it would cause a huge amount of damage, maybe even destroy our planet.

Weight loss.
A meteorite found in Oklahoma in 1970 weighed 21 pounds (10 kg). Scientists estimated that before it entered Earth's atmosphere and began to burn, it weighed 2 tons (2,000 pounds).

How many asteroids are there? About 3,460 asteroids in space have been identified and given names. Astronomers think there are as many as 30,000 asteroids orbiting in the 342-million-mile-wide *asteroid belt* between Mars and Jupiter. Many, many more probably exist, but they may be as small as sand grains.

SEER-ees

Asteroids very rarely strike the Earth but, when they do, they can cause a great deal of destruction. Meteorites are much smaller fragments of "space debris" and many more of them do hit our planet. Scientists estimate that about 24,000 meteorites weighing more than three-and-one-half ounces strike the Earth each year. Even more tiny particles called *cosmic dust* drift down out of space every year. This space dust adds about 100,000 tons to the planet's weight.

If you put your hand out of the window of a moving car, you can feel the density and resistance of the air as it rushes by. This is what slows objects down as they move through the atmosphere. Once a meteoroid enters the Earth's thicker atmosphere, it slows down and the friction causes it to get very hot and bright. The flash of light is called a meteor. Most smaller meteoroids quickly burn up in the few seconds before they reach the ground. We call them *shooting stars* if they come down at night.

More Record Holders to Discover

As the world around us changes, some record holders will change, too. Some already *are* changing, as organisms like whales become rare, while others, such as rats, become more abundant. Large glaciers are melting and getting smaller, which causes ocean levels to rise. And if the African elephant or the bumblebee bat become extinct, they will no longer be the world's largest and smallest land mammals.

The seas are deep and dark. What secrets do they hide? Are there strange birds and animals that still hide in the dense forests of Africa, South America, and Southeast Asia? There are surely other animals and plants living on Earth that we don't know about today.

What about the vast universe beyond our solar system? No one knows for sure where—or even if—the universe ends. We discover new things about the incredible world of outer space every year. Are there record holders on Mars, other planets, or on worlds much farther away?

One of the most important "down-to-earth" questions of the future is—how can we protect our woodlands, rain forests, wetlands, and deserts so that they will always provide a home for the plants and animals that depend on them? The answer to this question will come from *you*. And this may make you the most important record holder of all.

pen-tailed shrew
(*Ptilocercus lowii*)

Index of Record Holders

Mammals

Birds

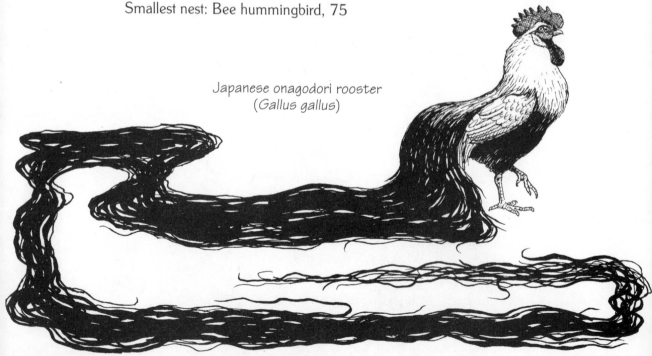

Japanese onagodori rooster
(*Gallus gallus*)

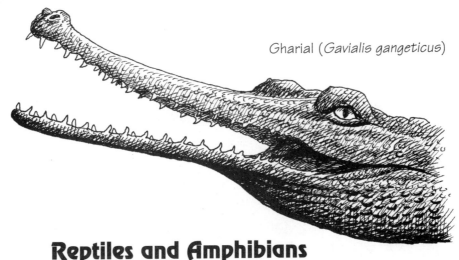

Gharial (*Gavialis gangeticus*)

Reptiles and Amphibians

Fishes

Haplochromis cichlid brooding its young in its mouth

Invertebrates

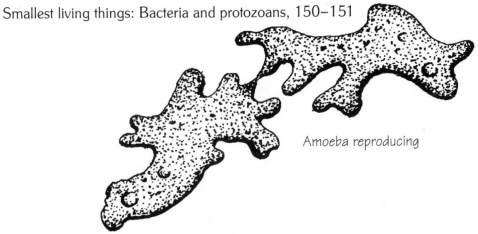

Amoeba reproducing

Plants

Earth and Space

Krakatua volcano

Index of Common Names
of Record Holders

Monarch butterfly

Blue arrow poison frogs compared to a quarter

northern pygmy mouse (Baiomys taylori)

O

P

R

S

Yak (*Bos grunniens*)

About the Author

As far as he knows, author and illustrator John R. Quinn hasn't set any world records of his own, but he has spent many years observing those in nature. An avid snorkeler and scuba diver, he has paddled about with whales, big fishes, and marine worms, and has studied eagle and hummingbird nests. He has kept electric catfish, tiny gobies, and sargassum fish in aquariums and has bred African cichlids —the fish that lay the fewest eggs of all. A huge marine toad once shared a jungle cabin with him in Trinidad, and he has been chased up a tree by the world's largest deer, the moose, in New Hampshire.

Quinn has written 11 books, including *Wildlife Survivors* (TAB–McGraw-Hill), *Fishwatching* and *Our Native Fishes* (The Countryman Press), *Fields of Sun and Grass: An Artist's Journal of the New Jersey Meadowlands* (Rutgers University Press), and *The Winter Woods* (Chatham Press), a Book of the Month Club Selection. He lives in New Jersey, which holds the record for the most densely populated state in the nation.